Indecent Exposures

Gwynne Edwards

Indecent Exposures
Buñuel, Saura, Erice & Almodóvar

Marion Boyars London • New York

Published in Great Britain and the United States
in 1995 by Marion Boyars Publishers
24 Lacy Road, London SW15 1NL
237 East 39th Street, New York NY 10016

Distributed in Australia and New Zealand by
Peribo Pty Ltd, Terrey Hills, NSW

British Library Cataloguing in Publication Data
Edwards, Gwynne
    Indecent Exposures: Buñuel, Saura, Erice & Almodóvar
    I. Title
    791.430922

Library of Congress Cataloging in Publication
Edwards, Gwynne.
    Indecent exposures: Buñuel, Saura, Erice & Almodóvar / Gwynne
Edwards.
    Includes bibliographical references (p.   )
    1. Motion pictures—Spain.   2. Motion picture producers and
directors—Spain.   I. Title.
    PN1993.5.S7E39   1994
    791.43'0233'092246—dc20   94–2998

ISBN 0–7145–2984–2 Original paperback

DS   T

Laserset in Palatino and Optima
by Ann Buchan (Typesetters), Middlesex
Printed in Great Britain by
Biddles Ltd,
Guildford and King's Lynn on acid-free paper

Contents

Preface   7
Introduction   9
Viridiana   26
The Exterminating Angel   41
Tristana   55
The Hunt   71
Raise Ravens   86
Carmen   101
Ay, Carmela!   116
The Spirit of the Beehive   132
The South   148
Matador   164
Women on the Verge of a Nervous
   Breakdown   181
High Heels   198
Conclusion   215
Bibliography   218
Index   221

Preface

In the last twenty-five years, the opportunities to see Spanish films in Britain and the United States have increased greatly, not least because of the proliferation of art-house cinemas, arts centres and university film clubs; not only the work of Luis Buñuel but also the films of Carlos Saura, Victor Erice and, most recently, Pedro Almodóvar are now being shown. However, despite Spain's fairly recent entry into the European Community and a much greater accessibility to the country than before 1975, it remains true that, historically and culturally, Spain is still for many a closed book. In the twentieth century the most significant events in Spanish history have been the Civil War of 1936 to 1939, and the transition from dictatorship to democracy in the last fifteen years. Both events have shaped the lives and the attitudes of Spaniards in general; a process which has been reflected in all the various art forms, including the cinema. The purpose of this book is to suggest, through the detailed examination of twelve significant films by the four directors in question, how they reflect the historical and cultural background of Spain today; to indicate the links, as well as the differences, between the four film-makers; and, of course, to reveal the fascination and the quality of the films themselves.

Every effort has been made by the author to trace the

current distributors of the films discussed in this study. This has proved an impossible task. The author has therefore decided to acknowledge the original distributors of the stills reproduced.

Introduction

In his autobiography, written in 1938, two years after the outbreak of the Spanish Civil War, Luis Buñuel observed of his childhood:

> My infancy slipped by in an almost mediaeval atmosphere (like that of nearly all the Spanish provinces) between my native town and Zaragoza. I feel it necessary to say here (since it explains in part the trend of the modest work which I later accomplished) that the two basic sentiments of my childhood, which stayed with me well into adolescence, are those of a profound eroticism, at first sublimated in a great religious faith, and a permanent consciousness of death. It would take too long here to analyze the reasons. It suffices that I was not an exception among my compatriots, since this is a very Spanish characteristic, and our art, exponent of the Spanish spirit, was impregnated with these two sentiments. The last civil war, peculiar and ferocious as no other, exposed them clearly.[1]

The observation is revealing in a variety of ways, pointing, as it does, to: a highly traditional and conservative way of life, barely changed for centuries; the importance, within those traditions, of religion and morality, and the way in which sexual feelings have been conditioned by them; the relevance of Buñuel's experience to many Spaniards; and the significance of the Spanish

Civil War as a period in which all these forces and characteristics were made evident as never before.

With the victory of the Nationalists and the beginning in 1939 of the Franco dictatorship that would last for thirty-six years, the kind of Spain described by Buñuel was one that was fervently championed by the state. The role of the Catholic Church, weakened in the years before the War, grew strong once more, firmly supported by the new regime. In conjunction with it, the traditional virtues of family life, including the role of woman as wife and mother, were greatly emphasized, and any deviation from the norm — such as homosexuality — frowned upon. In economic terms, the picture of post-Civil War Spain was one of recession and grinding poverty, of unemployment and hopes destroyed both in the cities and in the vast rural areas which had, in any case, always been extremely poor. Having left Spain before the outbreak of the War, Buñuel would not experience such conditions himself until 1960, when he returned to make *Viridiana*, and when in some ways things were beginning to improve. They were, however, precisely the circumstances into which Carlos Saura (1932–), Victor Erice (1940–), and Pedro Almodóvar (1949–) were born.[2] This being the case, it is not surprising to discover that the issues with which they deal in their films are very much those which preoccupied Buñuel. However, it is the strongly individual approach of these different directors to similar themes which provides their work with its enormous interest and vigour. In many ways the strength of Spanish cinema lies in its Spanishness: its concern with Spanish issues, its drawing on Spanish traditions, its essentially Spanish style. Its strength lies, in short, in the fact that it has been barely touched by Hollywood.

Born in 1900 in the small provincial town of Calanda, some fifty miles from Zaragoza, Luis Buñuel was the eldest child of well-to-do parents, enjoying a background of privilege against which he would later react. A rejection of traditional values was strongly developed in Buñuel well before he left Spain for Paris in 1925 and was therefore merely confirmed by his association with the Paris Surrealists when he joined the group in 1929. In Spain itself he had observed at first hand a way of life which he would later define in the following way:

> Morality — middle-class morality, that is — is for me immoral. One must fight it. It is a morality founded on our most unjust institutions — religion, fatherland, family culture — everything that people call the pillars of society.[3]

Buñuel's stance was in part political, reflecting a strongly left-wing attitude, and his reasons for joining the official Surrealist group may well have been its flirtation with the Communist Party: a desire to ally a revolution in consciousness to a concern with changing the material conditions in which people lived. On the other hand, Buñuel's view was simply that, as a consequence of centuries of religious and educational indoctrination and the development of a relatively fixed and inflexible social structure in the so-called civilized world, men and women had been progressively denied their freedom, in particular their capacity to give expression to their deepest and truest feelings. It is this inner, true reality which Buñuel and, of course, the Surrealists, believed was best revealed in dreams, in which subconscious urges and longings flood to the surface, unhindered by reason or conscience. It was this reality which was, for him, most denied in the bourgeoisie, fettered by hide-bound attitudes.

The essential themes of Buñuel's cinema are vividly set out in his first two films, the surrealist *Un Chien andalou* and *L'Age d'or* of 1929 and 1930. In a striking sequence in *Un Chien andalou*, the male protagonist's lustful advance on a young woman is thwarted by a great weight of grand pianos, priests and dead donkeys. Later in the film the two books held aloft by the now entirely passive young man become revolvers with which he shoots and kills another young man who has urged him to change his way of life. In the two sequences Buñuel reveals both graphically and wittily the inhibiting effects of culture, religion and education upon the individual. *L'Age d'or* develops these ideas in a more specific social context. The young and passionate lovers, Lya Lys and Gaston Modot, seek only to be together, to consummate their love, but are thwarted at every step by the bourgeois world to which they belong and from which they seek to free themselves. Much of the film is set in Rome, 'the Secular Seat of the Church'. Arriving at a dinner-party by car, the bourgeois guests are seen to carry religious objects with them. Later, suddenly conscious of her moral waywardness, Lya Lys abandons her passionate lover. If religious and moral values prevail, the dinner-party sequence also exposes good manners and social etiquette: women are treated with deference and respect and codes of conduct are strictly observed in a world in which appearance is all. This highly privileged bourgeois group is not, it might be argued, representative of society at large. On the other hand, Buñuel regarded it as embodying in a heightened form all those traditional values he had seen at work in France and Spain alike. And if both films were made before the Spanish war, they nevertheless embody precisely those values which existed in Spain at that time and which the Right would champion after Franco's triumph. *Un Chien andalou* was, and has remained, notorious for its opening sequence in which a razor-wielding Buñuel slices a young woman's eye. This and the depiction of scorpions at the beginning of *L'Age d'or* represent his attempt to awaken the bourgeoisie to its own complacency, the beginning of an all-out assault which the other directors discussed here would continue in their own particular way.

Buñuel's initial assault on the Church and on middle-class morality in general was one which he sustained throughout his long career. In *Nazarín*, made in Mexico in 1958, he exposes the futility of a priest's excessive Christian idealism in a harsh and selfish world and, in conjunction with it, the hypocrisy and sanctimoniousness of many of the representatives of the Catholic Church. Six years later, in *Simon of the Desert*, the holy man who spends fourteen years on top of a pillar in the name of his faith is ruthlessly mocked. As far as the bourgeoisie is concerned, the kind of world embodied in the drawing room sequences of *L'Age d'or*, with its emphasis on appearance, seemliness and propriety, is evoked in many other films, from *Diary of a Chambermaid*, made in 1963, where it forms the background, to *The Discreet Charm of the Bourgeoisie* of 1972, in which it is very much in the foreground. In both of them the surface of bourgeois life is stripped away to reveal the fears, anxieties and sexual hang-ups that derive from repression and inhibition.

When Buñuel returned to Spain in late 1960 in order to make *Viridiana*, the Franco dictatorship was twenty-one years old and the country virtually unchanged from the one he had left so many years ago. The religious values epitomized by the novice nun were everywhere apparent, as was the poverty and hunger represented by the beggars she seeks to help. It was a scenario which perfectly matched Buñuel's corrosive vision. Two years later *The Exterminating Angel*, although made in Mexico, focuses on a bourgeois group which in its attitudes is as much Spanish as Mexican, allowing Buñuel to expose those concerns with appearance, name, social status and the like, which, in a right-wing regime such as Franco's, were entirely opposed to the interests of the common people. In *Tristana*, made in Spain in 1969, its action set in Toledo in the years preceding the outbreak of the Civil War, he concentrated in particular on the role and place of woman in a society dominated by traditional attitudes.

Buñuel's cinematic style is, despite his uniqueness, characteristic of the style of Spanish cinema as a whole. Partly because of financial strictures, partly because of his own tastes, his manner is simple, direct and austere. His Mexican films, most of them made quickly and on a very limited budget, encouraged a style which was itself economical. There are very few tricks and none of the gimmickry we associate with American films — overhead shots, bizarre angles and the like. Always assisting the narrative, pushing it forward quickly and clearly, Buñuel's cinematic style has been vividly compared to the precise and quick art of hanging wall-paper.[4]

In complete contrast, Carlos Saura has spent his entire life in Spain. Born in Huesca in 1932, the son of a government official, he spent most of the Civil War years in Republican held areas, in particular Madrid and Barcelona, where his father had been sent. The War itself made a very powerful impression on him, as he has himself observed:

I recall my childhood very well, and in a sense I
believe that the War must have marked me more
than I thought. It is perhaps the period of my life
that I remember most clearly: the songs from the
war, the children's games, the bombings, the black-
outs, the hunger, the dead. . . . If for Proust his
childhood was a series of more or less poetic
details in a family environment, for me those memories are much more violent: a bomb which fell on
my school, a blood-stained child with glass in her
face. . . .[5]

These were memories which Saura would incorporate
in several of his films, such as the episode of the
bombing of the school at the beginning of *Cousin Angélica*,
made in 1973 and, of course, *Ay, Carmela!*, which is set
during the war itself and which features so many of the
songs referred to by Saura.

Although his childhood was marked by memories of
particular incidents in the War, Saura's adult life was
coloured, like that of all Spaniards, by what is known in
Spanish as the *posguerra*, the post-war period, and by
all that this represented. It was, firstly, a period in
which the terrible violence perpetrated during the War
by Nationalists and Republicans alike left its long
shadow. Fear, uncertainty and hatred prevailed on the
losing side; arrogance, intolerance and a sense of superiority on the winning side. In terms of social structures
and attitudes, the Franco dictatorship favoured throughout its thirty-six year existence the conservative
middle-class. It represented all the traditional values
for which Franco himself stood and which he sought to
inculcate at the expense of those who had fought against
him: the working-class and the intellectuals. In addition, the Franco period encouraged myth: the myth

that the War had been a crusade; the myth of Spanish *machismo* — a sexual chauvinism which stemmed directly from Franco's championing of political and national chauvinism; and the myth of the family within which the role of woman as loyal wife and dedicated mother was clearly defined. And behind all this, supporting Franco both during the War and after, was the Catholic Church, a powerful influence on the education of children and on the moral attitudes of Spaniards throughout their lives. This is the background in which Saura's films are deeply rooted.[6]

The violence that was the aftermath of the War, a deep scar on the Spanish mentality, acquires particular force in *The Hunt*, made in 1965, in which three of the hunters have fought in, and been marked by, the War, but it is equally evident in other films. Twenty-two years later, in *El Dorado*, Saura would embody the kind of violence perpetrated in the War in the figure of Lope de Aguirre who, in 1560, set out to discover 'El Dorado' and who, in the process, slaughtered many of his companions, as well as thousands of South American Indians. As far as traditional values are concerned, they lie at the heart of *Raise Ravens*, made in 1975, in which a detailed picture of a middle-class family is presented and in which, in true Buñuelian manner, the façade of good manners and propriety is stripped away to expose an underbelly of frustration, philandering, infidelity and treachery. This and other films, like *Ana and the Wolves*, made in 1972, reveal the effects too of a Francoist education and environment on the children of the family. At the end of *Ana and the Wolves* the three sons of a harsh and tyrannical mother proceed to exercise their frustration on Ana, the governess, by cutting her hair, raping her and shooting her dead.

While many of Saura's films portray the violence of

male behaviour, the theme of the Spanish male stereo-
type acquires particular force in *Carmen*, made in 1983.
Here the effect of placing the traditional story of Don
José and Carmen side by side with a contemporary
story involving a modern Carmen and her lover Antonio
is to reveal that the age-old Spanish male's view of his
own superiority and of woman's inferior station, which
were both heightened during the dictatorship, has not
changed in the post-Franco period. In his 1981 adaptation of Lorca's famous play, *Blood Wedding*, Saura
portrayed a society concerned with name, honour and
the traditional roles of men and women, whose values,
going back beyond the beginning of the Civil War, still
largely exist in the late twentieth century. As for the
role of woman, the figure of Carmen — independent,
wilful, assertive — is no less than a role model for the
new Spanish woman. It is significant that her modern
embodiment is murdered by her jealous and intolerant
lover at the end of the film.

While Saura's cinema is rooted in the kind of issues
and concerns described above, they are rarely presented simply in black and white political terms. In
fact, Saura has denied that his work is primarily political: 'If I were essentially political, I wouldn't make
films but dedicate myself to another activity where
politics could play a greater part'.[7] His films are complex, his characters driven by emotions and impulses
— desire, frustration, fear, guilt, jealousy, repression,
fetishes — which they often fail to understand. To this
extent there is a strong Freudian influence and, beyond
that, a clear link between Saura and Buñuel. A true
disciple of the older film director, Saura is fascinated
by the inner lives of his characters and by the complex
processes that make them what they are. But these
processes are linked to, and exacerbated by, the society

in which the characters live and are therefore a comment on Francoism itself.

Saura's cinematic style owed something at first to
Italian Neo-realism, so influential in the 1940s and
1950s. Even then, however, it differed from it: in *The
Hunt*, a realistic framework is used selectively and
symbolically to extend the range of the film's meaning,
and as much emphasis is placed on the characters'
inner lives as on their activities. In later films the
structure itself becomes more complex, as in the case of
Raise Ravens, where flashbacks and leaps in time create
an often bewildering effect which perfectly evokes the
world of memory. Also in *Carmen* the shifts between
the traditional and the contemporary stories are often
achieved in a way which makes the distinction between
the one and the other quite impossible to detect. In
terms of style and technique, Saura's films reveal a
steady and complex development. He is undoubtedly
one of the most fascinating Spanish film-makers in
relation both to the concerns of his films and to their
visual language.[8]

Of the four film directors considered here, Victor
Erice is by far the most mysterious, a figure shrouded in
anonymity. In the words of one Spanish writer, 'He is
virtually unknown, the most "secret" of Spanish film-
makers'.[9] Born in San Sebastián in 1940, eight years
younger than Saura, Erice likewise experienced a childhood over which the Civil War cast its long, dark shadow.
He has himself observed: '. . . civil war is the most
terrible experience a community can live through because brother is set against brother. In a civil war
everyone is defeated — there are no real victors. What
characterizes those people in my memory of my childhood is that they were in general very silent, introspective
people. They didn't want to speak because they had

lived through something so horrific. We children experienced it as a form of absence: we sensed that deep down they were far away. And perhaps that is why there was a lack of communication.'[10] Two of Erice's three films — *The Spirit of the Beehive* and *The South*, made in 1973 and 1983 respectively — are concerned with children and with the effect of growing up both during and after the War. Inasmuch as they depict a world in which there is great economic hardship, in which people's dreams and ambitions are doomed, in which husbands and wives are driven apart by disillusionment, and in which children are marked by it all, we may conclude, in the absence of factual information, that this was the world in which Erice himself grew up. Secondly, the north of Spain, not least the Basque country, was fiercely anti-Franco, and there can be no doubt that these two films in particular take a similar, albeit oblique, political stance. It is no accident that Frankenstein's monster should dominate *The Spirit of the Beehive*, its action set in 1940, or that *The South*, set in the post-War years, should suggest a country divided.

As far as the issues so central to the *posguerra* are concerned, few characterize Erice's work in the way that they do Saura's. The middle class, as we see it in *Raise Ravens*, for example, does not figure in either *The Spirit of the Beehive* or *The South*. The former is set in a poor village in Castile, the latter in a rather more prosperous household in the north, but neither film explores those traditional values and attitudes exposed so clearly by Buñuel and Saura. Nor do the issues of machismo and the role of woman really figure in Erice's work. If there is one theme which links Saura and Erice, it is the theme of violence, although Erice treats it in a very different way. In *The Hunt* and *El Dorado*, for example, Saura presents violence as something which, if inherent in the

Spanish character, is exacerbated by war, manifesting itself in brutal acts committed against people and animals alike. The violence in Erice's films is altogether different: the violence which the War has done to people's lives in terms of its disruption of their hopes, the destruction of their ideals and their capacity for love and communication. It is thus an unseen, silent, corrosive violence which, affecting parents, affects in turn their children, scarring them emotionally as they grow up and are shaped by what they see and feel.

The emphasis on inner rather than external violence points to Erice's preoccupation with the inner lives of his characters, and this accounts for the quiet, subdued, unostentatious quality of his work. In this respect the physical world of Erice's films is all important, but only in the sense that the things and objects on which attention is focused are important in relation to the inner lives of his characters. The dark and often empty rooms and corridors of the house in *The Spirit of the Beehive* evoke the empty lives of the characters; the darkness of night the fears of the child, Ana; and the Frankenstein monster, the fearful presence that her father sometimes becomes. If in one direction Erice's cinematic style is based on a realism as simple, direct and clear-cut as Buñuel's, in another it is highly stylized. There are no tricks or gimmicks, but aspects of the real world are carefully selected in order to create for the viewer a point of entry into the characters' lives.

Pedro Almodóvar, born in 1949 in Ciudad Real, grew up in extremely humble circumstances. His father was a muleteer responsible for transporting wine to the town of Jaén. The provincial society in which Almodóvar spent his childhood was both highly traditional and economically backward. Thinking that the priesthood would prove a suitable career for him, his parents sent him to a school run by priests in the town of Cáceres, an experience which clearly gave him an insight into the religious life. In 1966, however, and against the wishes of his parents, the seventeen-year old Almodóvar went to live in Madrid.

The second half of the 1960s, less than ten years before Franco's death, was a time in which the regime, still oppressive in many respects, was seeking to give Spain a new, modern image. The influence of pop music, particularly British, was strongly felt. Hippies began to make their appearance in Madrid. The drug scene developed for the first time. During the first half of the 1970s, with Franco an increasingly sick old man, the process of opposition to the old traditions and values continued to grow. With his death everything changed fundamentally. The new liberty meant, in many respects, that 'anything goes', entirely under-standable in relation to the restrictions of the past. For the younger generation fashion has become all-impor-tant; there is little restriction placed on soft-porn publications; sexual freedom is embraced with enthu-siasm; the old prejudices against gay people, although still strong, cannot prevent such groups expressing themselves. At the time of Franco's death, Almodóvar was twenty-six years old, much influenced by the new trends and therefore thoroughly representative of the new Spain.

Almodóvar's concerns as a film-maker are evident from the very beginning. During the 1970s, availing himself of a friend's Super 8 camera and making short films for himself and his companions, he produced such titles as *Two Whores, or a Love Story which Ends in Marriage, The Fall of Sodom* (both 1974), *The Dream or the Star* (1975), and *Sex, Easy Come Easy Go* (1977). What is interesting about these early films, the majority no longer than fifteen minutes in duration, is that Almodóvar had complete control over them, something which he has striven to maintain to a large extent in his later commercial films. They were also comic films in which his main purpose was to entertain. The comic purpose, however, which is such an integral part of much of Almodóvar's later cinema, was achieved by the use of subject matter which, in the Spain of the time, was entirely subversive: transvestism, gay relationships, etc. The concerns and style of these early films can be seen to much better effect in Almodóvar's first professional film, *Pepi, Luci, Bom and All the Other Girls on the Heap*, made between 1979 and 1980. Its heroine, Pepi, is raped at the outset by an evil and lustful policeman. Bent on revenge, she hires her friends to beat him up but succeeds only in beating up his identical twin brother. Pepi subsequently sets about corrupting the policeman's wife, Luci, by introducing her and her sadistic girl friend Bom to a way of life, which she has never known before. By the end of the film Luci's own masochistic tendencies have been released, and she returns to her husband who, much to her own satisfaction, proceeds to beat her regularly. If the outline of the story seems rather grim, its treatment by Almodóvar is entirely comic, its effect often hilarious, as in the case of a competition entitled 'General Erections', which is his joking reference to the General Elections of 1977. Nothing could be further removed from those erstwhile values of the dictatorship. However, the difference between Almodóvar and the other, older film-directors considered here is that he, instead of questioning those values and exposing them for what they are, presents an entirely different world. It is, in a way, a measure of the extent to which this alternative world is now recognized and largely accepted that Almodóvar's films are themselves received so warmly by so many. As Almodóvar has himself observed of *Pepi, Luci, Bom . . .*: 'It is as if life is really like this. As if women are really like this: they are completely free.'[11]

Since *Pepi, Luci, Bom . . .*, Almodóvar has made eight films in which his treatment of gay relationships, male and female, transvestism and the like are very much to the fore, and in which his typically subversive humour is prominent. They are also films whose style reveals Almodóvar's constant cultural influences: the tradition of the photo-novel, comics, pop music and pop art, the world of fashion, and Hollywood films of the 1940s and 1950s give them a very modern appearance. They are full of the bright colours, patterns and objects of the world we live in; a world of airports, discos, television studios, advertising, fashion-houses, clubs, apartments and city streets. It is a world and a style which seem very far removed from the much more austere world presented by Buñuel in his Spanish films, but it would be wrong to take this conclusion too far. If Almodóvar's world is an alternative to that represented in the work of these other film-makers, it is bound to reflect that other world too. And in so doing, Almodóvar depicts its representatives — priests, policemen, bourgeois types in general — as subversively as do his predecessors, and with an ironic tone frequently reminiscent of Buñuel. If, therefore, Almodóvar represents a break with the past in one way, he is in another a continuation of it.[12]

Notes

1. See Francisco Aranda, *Luis Buñuel: A Critical Biography*, trans. David Robinson, London: Secker and Warburg, 1975, p. 12.

2. For a detailed account of Spanish history during the period in question, see Raymond Carr, *Modern Spain, 1875–1980*, Oxford: Oxford University Press, 1980. For the post-Franco period, see John Hooper, *The Spaniards: a Portrait of the New Spain*, Harmondsworth: Penguin Books, 1986.

3. See Donald Richie, 'The Moral Code of Luis Buñuel', in *The World of Luis Buñuel, Essays in Criticism*, ed. Joan Mellen, New York: Oxford University Press, 1978, p. 111.

4. David Robinson, 'Luis Buñuel and *Viridiana*', in *The World of Luis Buñuel . . .*, p. 240. For detailed studies of Buñuel's cinema, the reader is recommended to Freddy Buache, *The Cinema of Luis Buñuel*, trans. Peter Graham, London and New York: Tantivy-Barnes, 1973; Raymond Durgnat, *Luis Buñuel*, London: Studio Vista, 1967; Gwynne Edwards, *The Discreet Art of Luis Buñuel*, London and Boston: Marion Boyars, 1982; Ado Kyrou, *Luis Buñuel*, Paris: Edition Seghers, 1962; Virginia Higginbotham, *Luis Buñuel*, Boston: Twayne, 1979; Agustin Sánchez Vidal, *Luis Buñuel*, Madrid: Ediciones JC, 1984.

5. See Agustin Sánchez Vidal, *El cine de Carlos Saura*, Zaragoza: Caja de Ahorros de la Inmaculada, 1988, p. 13. The translation into English is my own.

6. There are informative sections on the social and cultural characteristics of the Franco period and afterwards in John Hopewell, *Out of the Past: Spanish Cinema after Franco*, London: British Film Institute, 1986.

7. See John Hopewell, *Out of the Past* . . ., p. 136.

8. For general studies of Saura's films, see Agustin Sánchez Vidal, *El cine de Carlos Saura* . . .; Enrique Brasó, *Carlos Saura*, Madrid: Taller Ediciones JB, 1974; Manuel Hidalgo, *Carlos Saura*, Madrid: Ediciones JC, 1981; Marcel Oms, *Carlos Saura*, Paris: Edilig, 1981.

9. In Angel A. Pérez Gómez and José L. Martínez Montalbán, *Cine Español 1951–1978*, Bilbao: Ediciones Mensajero, 1978.

10. In an interview with Rikki Morgan, *Sight and Sound*, Spring 1993, p. 27.

11. Quoted in Francisco Blanco, 'Boquerini', *Pedro Almodóvar*, Madrid: Ediciones JC, 1989, p. 33.

12. As well as the above, the reader is recommended to María Antonia García de León and Teresa Maldonado, *Pedro Almodóvar, la otra españa cañí*, Ciudad Real: Biblioteca de autores y temas manchegos, 1989, and Nuria Vidal, *El cine de Pedro Almodóvar*, Barcelona: Ediciones Destino, 1988.

Viridiana

Viridiana, made in Spain in 1961, illustrates particularly well Buñuel's famous assertion that sex without religion is like an egg without salt. It was the film's heady mixture of religion and eroticism, culminating in the attempted rape of a young woman who had earlier trained to become a nun, which, after its first showing at Cannes on May 17, 1961, so enraged the Vatican and the Spanish authorities. *L'Osservatore Romano* made great play of the film's elements of blasphemy and sacrilege, while in Spain General Franco ordered copies to be seized and forbade all reference to *Viridiana*'s winning of the Palme d'or at Cannes. The controversy which had surrounded the première of *L'Age d'or* in Paris in 1930, inciting attacks on the cinema and leading to the banning of the film by the chief of police, attended Buñuel once more. For his own part, he claimed that it was never his intention to be blasphemous, although it is always prudent to take Buñuel's statements with a pinch of salt. What cannot be denied is that the close association of religion and eroticism is something which preoccupied him in more than one film, and that his own fascination with it reflects a paradox which lies at the very heart of the Spanish tradition.

These references to eroticism and religion, so ingrained in Buñuel's childhood, were later to find an even more specific echo in his comments on the making of *Viridiana*:

her back on the world. Struck by his niece's remarkable resemblance to his wife, who died in his arms on their wedding-night and whose memory he has worshipped ever since with an almost religious devotion, Don Jaime's repressed sexual feelings are slowly awakened. Having persuaded Viridiana to wear his wife's wedding-dress, he fails to persuade her to marry him, drugs her, lays her on the bed and, while she is unconscious, is tempted to rape her. Prevented from doing so by a pang of conscience, he subsequently makes her believe he has taken her by force and, when she rejects him again and leaves the house, he hangs himself.

The religious theme, and in particular the notion of spirituality, is evoked poignantly in both Viridiana and Don Jaime. Our first glimpse of her in the film's opening sequence emphasizes the whiteness of her habit and the pale perfection of her face, the external manifestation of an innocence and purity as yet untouched by the sinfulness of the world outside the convent. This initial image, with all its associations, is then developed in a number of key sequences in Don Jaime's house. As she undresses in her bedroom, the whiteness of her habit becomes the whiteness of her underclothing, the paleness of her face, her bare thigh. Just afterwards we see her sleepwalking, the whole sequence imbued with an ethereal, spiritual quality which is derived from her mechanical, almost floating movement, the religious music which accompanies it, and from the whiteness of her long nightdress. But this beautiful vision is in turn superceded by that of Viridiana dressed in the wedding-gown of Don Jaime's dead wife. When she appears in the corridor of the vast and gloomy house, dressed in the bridal gown and carrying a candelabra, the image is again one of purity, innocence and virginity. Later, when Don Jaime lays her on

the bed, she reminds us in her stillness and her whiteness of one of those religious statues to be found in
Spanish churches. The sheen of the dress, the repose of
the figure and the calm of the face create a wonderful
sense of spirituality. In addition, this evocation of other-
worldliness is heightened throughout this part of the
film by shots of the religious objects — the cross, the
nails, the crown of thorns — which Viridiana brings
with her.

As for Don Jaime, his house has become, since the
death of his wife, a cathedral to her memory, the equivalent of Viridiana's convent. At night it is filled with the
sound of sacred music, played either by himself on the
harmonium or in the form of gramophone records.
Furthermore, the dead woman's clothing, preserved
by Don Jaime, has become over the years the equivalent of religious relics, gazed upon, touched, even worn
by him in a kind of sacred ritual; the counterpart of
Viridiana's religious objects. When she assumes the
bridal gown, she becomes in effect a reincarnation of
the dead woman and, as he gazes at her on the bed, the
candles around it suggest a shrine at which he wor-
ships.

The theme of spirituality is, nevertheless, closely
interwoven with a powerful eroticism, for although
Viridiana is a novice nun, she is also a beautiful woman,
and nothing suggests this teasing paradox more than
Buñuel's own phrase: 'chaste eroticism'. The ambiguity is perfectly captured in the sequence in which she
removes her stockings: the whiteness of her thighs
suggests an innocent perfection, but it also contains an
enormous sexual allure. The reality of a woman who
belongs to the world of the spirit but is also very much
of the flesh is captured neatly in the words of Don
Jaime's astute servant, Ramona: '. . . her rough night-

gown must chaff her delicate skin.'[3] If, however,
Viridiana is unaware of her physical effect on others, it
is something which step by step ensnares Don Jaime. In
his devotion to his wife's garments, which include her
underwear, there is a strong sexual undercurrent, the
sense of a passion unfulfilled for which the feel of what
lay next to her skin is a form of compensation.[4] The
attempt to keep passion alive, as touching as it is
pathetic, becomes increasingly, through Viridiana's presence, a fire that blazes dangerously into life. The
sleep-walking sequence, ethereal in its way, also allows Don Jaime to gaze at Viridiana's exposed thighs.
When he persuades her to wear his wife's bridal gown,
the innocent intended bride of Christ becomes the
living form of his own bride that was. As she lies on the
marriage bed in Don Jaime's bedroom, the religious
and spiritual associations of the sequence teasingly vie
with worldly and basic instincts. She is, in effect, both
Virgin and virgin, saint and temptress, spirit and flesh.
When Don Jaime takes her in his arms, her arched body
emphasizes the upward thrust of her breasts and when,
further tempted, he undoes the buttons of the bridal
dress, it is not the whiteness of innocence which confronts him but the naked flesh of a dazzlingly attractive
young woman.

When, distraught by Viridiana's departure, Don Jaime
hangs himself from a tree, he does so with the skipping
rope he had earlier given to Rita, Ramona's small
daughter. The shot of the hanging body gives particular emphasis to the rope's phallus-like handles and
therefore to the way in which Don Jaime's surrender to
sexual temptation has, through guilt, brought about
his suicide. In this context, the rope is one of many
physical objects in the film — crosses, thorns, legs, feet
— which are used to define particular lives and atti-

tudes within the context of the two themes of religion and eroticism.[5] The rope appears for the first time in an early sequence in which Rita is seen skipping: the camera focuses on her quickly moving feet and legs, while her hands firmly grip the skipping rope handles. The emphasis falls, of course, on her lack of inhibition and her innocence in sexual matters. Later we see Rita and Viridiana skipping together, which not only underlines the innocence of both but also draws attention to what ought to be the difference between a child and an adult woman. In Viridiana, however, maturity has not brought sexual knowledge or experience, only ignorance and fear. When the phallus motif occurs again in the form of a cow's teat which Rita urges her to grasp firmly, Viridiana cannot bring herself to do so, her deep-seated fears disguised in nervous laughter. Later on in the film the discarded rope will be used as a belt by one of the beggars to whom Viridiana shows compassion, its practical use in this instance a pointer to the man's pragmatic approach to life. In this particular sense the world of the convent and the beggars are at opposite extremes, literally worlds apart, and, with Don Jaime's death, Viridiana stands uneasily between them. Convinced by her uncle that he has raped her, even though he then denies it, she believes she cannot return to the convent. The rest of the film is therefore an account of her experience of the world, first in relation to Jorge, Don Jaime's illegitimate son, and then in relation to the beggars. In both, the conflict of the spirit and the flesh acquires even more varied forms.

Unlike his father, Jorge has no sexual guilt or inhibitions.[6] In the first place, when he inherits his father's house, he brings with him his mistress, Lucía, and has no scruples about installing her in his father's bed, previously so revered by the old man. A shot of Jorge's

feet in a bowl of steaming water, linking and contrasting with earlier shots of Viridiana's feet, knees and
thighs, is intended to present him as a man of the world
who, in order to see what improvements can be made,
has spent the day tramping his derelict estate. A significant moment occurs when he informs Viridiana
that he wishes to modernize the old house and, in
particular, to install electricity: 'The house. I want to
put light in it.'

Jorge's advocacy of progress contrasts markedly with
Viridiana who, just prior to this, has been praying in
her convent-like room, surrounded by her religious
objects. She may have left the convent behind physically but otherwise carries its baggage with her:
monasticism set in the modern world. Her exposure to
it, as well as her efforts to avoid contamination, are
sugested by the smoke from Jorge's cigar that drifts
across the room. She can no more avoid it than his
teasing eyeing of her body and, when he has gone, her
opening of the window to clear the smoke is also a
meaningful perspective on the world outside, which
now confronts her.

The true reality of this world is revealed further in
Jorge's sexual pragmatism. Tiring of her situation and
annoyed by his interest in Viridiana, Lucía decides to
leave, and draws from Jorge an entirely matter-of-fact
reaction: 'That's life. Some people come together, others split up. What can we do if that's the way things
are?'

Quite soon, moreover, he replaces her with the servant, Ramona. In the attic where they first embrace, its
junk and debris present an image of the wreckage of
Don Jaime's wasted life, a cat pounces on an unsus-
pecting rat. It is a shot which encapsulates Buñuel's
view that the world must be accepted for what it is in all

its imperfection. At the end of *Nazarín* the disillusioned priest accepts a pineapple from a peasant woman, his tears of gratitude born of a recognition not of God but of man. It is a lesson which Viridiana will begin to learn.

If Jorge is part of the lesson, the beggars complete it. Here indeed is an image of 'the world' in all its ugliness worthy of Breughel, Bosch or Goya. In rural Spain, as Buñuel observed of his childhood in Calanda, there was often a distinctly medieval feel, not least in terms of physical deformity, and in the group of beggars he has put together there is a visually striking collection of individuals: Poca, a small, large-nosed, toothless busy-body, as quick in his movements as a rat; blind Amalio, stocky, coarse-featured, his eyes disturbingly off-centre in their sockets; Enedina, Amalio's woman, bony, angular, her body thin and scrawny; the 'leproso', tall, gawky, lisping through missing teeth, his arm covered with open running sores. As Viridiana, taking pity on them, leads them to Don Jaime's house, they present a powerful image of a shambling, stumbling humanity struggling through the world on sticks and crutches. Nothing could be further removed, in physical terms, from the flawless beauty of Viridiana herself; a contrast which is further developed in moral terms.

The beggars can be said, with some degree of truth, to exemplify the seven deadly sins, in particular sloth, lust and gluttony. In presenting their experience in the house, culminating in the banquet and the dance, Buñuel seems almost to be putting on the screen the centre-piece of one of those Dutch triptychs — Bosch's *The Garden of Earthly Delights* comes to mind — in which the pleasures of the world are vividly displayed.[7] Given the centrality of sex in the film, it is given particular attention here. Amalio's lust for Enedina is much in evidence. As the beggars eat their first meal, he gropes her thighs and whispers into her ear. Later, unknown at first to Amalio, Poca makes love to Enedina behind the sofa in the dining room. At a given moment here, the camera picks out their protruding legs and in so doing recalls earlier shots of feet, knees and thighs, especially Viridiana's. The beggars' groping is, in a way, grotesque — the instant satisfaction of a pressing need as great as that which leads them to stuff their mouths with food — but Buñuel's point is that it is honest and real. To that extent it is preferable to the repressed and guilt-ridden passion of Don Jaime, which has led to his suicide, as well as to Viridiana's turning away from all things sexual. Indeed, her resolve to accommodate the beggars indicates that this is the reality from which she cannot turn away but must now increasingly accept.

It is her contact with the beggars, juxtaposing completely opposing values and attitudes, which gives this central section of the film its wonderful sense of irony, of the kind which Cervantes had exploited so successfully three and a half centuries earlier in a similar clash of idealism and practicality. In *Nazarín* Buñuel had been well aware of his visionary priest's literary antecendent as he travelled the roads of Spain accompanied by two women, one a prostitute: 'There goes Don Quixote with his two Sanchos'.[8] Viridiana is a figure in the same tradition, a female Quixote obsessed not so much with knights as with saints, and the spectacle is often just as comic.

Typical is the sequence of the painting of the Virgin. The lame beggar paints a religious scene — a sick woman lying on a bed, with the Virgin and two angels at her side. The subject matter of the picture is, of course, the subject matter of the film: Viridiana's attempt to 'heal' the beggars. The painting also suggests the sentimentality which is part of the tradition of religious painting, making the characters and events somehow divorced from life. It is brought down to earth, however, by the grotesque reality of the woman who acts as a model for the Virgin; the plain, pregnant and unsentimental Refugio, her name itself ironic in the context of her unwelcoming appearance and attitudes. She can only complain about her lack of comfort, while Poca adds his own malicious comments, 'She's no idea who the child's father was. She said it was night and she couldn't see his face.' The painting depicts a miracle. Viridiana's hopes of similarly 'healing' the beggars merely makes us smile.

Other incidents fill out the picture. Viridiana's compassion towards the 'leproso' is countered by the workmen who tie a can to his leg, fearful of the disease he may transmit to them. It is not so much that they are cruel or heartless, more that a concern with self-preservation is a fact of life. If we, like Viridiana, feel a certain sympathy for the 'leproso', constantly put-upon by his fellow men, we should also bear in mind Poca's observation, surely not entirely false, that the 'leproso', infected by a woman, places his arm in the holy water in church thereby infecting others. In a later incident we see him pick up an injured dove and tend to it affectionately, but later still the bird's feathers spill from his jacket, placing what seemed compassion in a totally different perspective. Without doubt one of the many triumphs of this film is the way in which a detailed picture of human beings and their attitudes and actions is constructed step by step, a picture which is never simple but fascinating in its complexity.

One of the key episodes in the middle section of the film is undoubtedly that in which Viridiana leads the beggars in prayer while workmen are renovating part of the house. Cutting rapidly in a series of alternating shots from prayer to physical work — from a line of the prayer to the sawing of wood, the slopping of water, a hammer breaking stone, etc — Buñuel encapsulates in a few moments the film's central theme. The way in which the prayer is interrupted by the sounds of the workmen reveals that the impact of the world at large is inescapable. Indeed, the sequence is so structured that the sounds of work acquire, in relation to the chanting of the prayer, the character of a response, which in a slightly different way may be seen as the unsentimental response of the world to religious idealism.

The climactic section of the film, the beggars' feast, enunciates this theme more powerfully still, and although Viridiana is not present, does so in ways which constantly bring her to mind. The white unblemished tablecloth on the long dining table evokes her habit, her underclothing, the bridal gown, and, of course, her purity. A quick transition reveals it stained with wine and, as the camera moves along the table, covered in the debris of the beggars' meal. This physical wreckage has its counterpoint in the gross, drunken, abusive and gesticulating figures of the beggars themselves.

The famous, or infamous, 'Last Supper' frame articulates in a brilliantly concise single image the gulf between, as Buñuel sees it, the world of Viridiana and the beggars. As the beggars pose to be 'photographed' by Enedina, they assume the postures of Christ and the disciples in Leonardo's 'La Cena'. Simultaneously, this grotesque image deliberately evokes the ideals of Christianity and the gross reality of the beggars which undermines it. One can imagine the outrage caused by this shot when the film was first screened, but Buñuel's purpose was clearly not blasphemous: it was merely to suggest that, just as in the photograph the beggars obliterate saintly virtues, they will also destroy Viridiana's compassion towards them.[9]

In the brilliant 'dance' sequence, evocations of the earlier part of the film return in a form both grotesque and hilarious. The 'leproso' appears from another room dressed in the corsets and bridal-veil. Accompanied by Poca and others, including a dwarf, he begins to perform a flamenco dance to the strains of the *Hallelujah Chorus*. The garments and the music recall Don Jaime's worship of his wife's memory, as well as the world of the convent and Viridiana as the intended bride of Christ; but it does so in a way which confronts that image of sanctity with another of the moral and spiritual ugliness of mankind. However, the sounds of Handel's music, as well as the evident pleasure of the participants, give this sequence a celebratory quality in which we, the audience, also take delight. When Amalio, informed of Enedina's infidelity with Poca, smashes the table and its contents with his flailing stick, the scene ends in violence, bringing to mind Buñuel's observation that we do not live in the best of possible worlds.[10]

The film's final sequences brings Viridiana herself to an acceptance of what she finally knows she cannot escape. Returning to the house with Jorge, she is seized by one of the beggars who attempts to rape her after Jorge has been knocked unconscious. In a shockingly revealing moment her fingers grasp the phallic handles of the skipping rope, which the beggar uses as a belt, and she faints, her earlier distaste provoked by the cow's teat now transformed into a true sexual fear. But with it comes final realization that if she had previously been born again in a Christian sense, she must, in order to live in the world, be born again to the world. Indeed, to continue the religious parallel, she is 'saved' here not by her Christian beliefs and values but by Jorge who, recovering consciousness, bribes the 'leproso' into battering the rapist into submission. In short, it is the practical and pragmatic Jorge, an expert in the ways of the world, who proves to be her saviour and deliverer.

The ending of the film points to a new beginning. Earlier associations are evoked in order to be rejected. Our first encounter with Viridiana after the attempted rape reveals her to be quite changed. A close-up of her face displays its whiteness and perfection and is therefore reminiscent of earlier moments in the film, but whiteness points now not to spirituality but to physical beauty, and when she looks at herself in a mirror she does so with a Narcissus-like absorption, as if aware for the first time of her physical attraction. Her hair too hangs loose around her shoulders, and it is clear that she has let her hair down in more ways than one. Outside, meanwhile, Rita has thrown Viridiana's crown of thorns onto a bonfire, signifying the end of her past way of life. Inside the house Viridiana makes her way to Jorge's room and joins him and Ramona as a record joyfully plays a tune whose refrain is, 'shake your cares away'. To what extent she will succeed in doing that is a question that remains unanswered. The expressions on the faces of the two women suggest uncertainty and suspicion, even hostility, but that is life and it has to be accepted on its own terms.

Of the greatness of *Viridiana* as a film there can be no doubt. Freddy Buache considers it to be a masterpiece, comparable with *L'Age d'or*. Francisco Aranda has observed that it is one of Buñuel's greatest achievements. What cannot be denied is that, in terms of its visual imagery, it is both rich and beautifully orchestrated, and it also has that sense of pace and flow which seems to be perfectly judged and which is so characteristic of Buñuel at his very best.[11] But in the end *Viridiana* is most noteworthy, perhaps, for the complexity and ambiguity of characters who, far from knowing each other, barely know themselves. To that extent *Viridiana* is a film of discovery, exemplified above all in Viridiana's growing awareness both of the world at large and of the hidden depths within herself. And beyond that, Buñuel's elegant stripping of Viridiana's soul is also an exposure of our own phobias and inhibitions, the cinema screen a mirror in which we watch ourselves.

Notes

1. Luis Buñuel, 'On *Viridiana*', in *The World of Luis Buñuel, Essays in Criticism*, ed. Joan Mellen, New York: Oxford University Press, 1978, p. 217.

2. 'Song of the Flame of Living Love.'

3. The close-ups of Viridiana's thighs and legs may be compared with similar shots in other films — Marta in *Los olvidados*, Tristana, and Séverine in *Belle de Jour*. Buñuel uses the camera in this context as the equivalent of a male eye, focussing on the woman in precisely the way that an admiring man does.

4. See Raymond Durgnat, *Luis Buñuel*, London: Studio Vista, 1967, p. 124: 'The erotic transvestite is, basically, seeking to console himself for the loss of a beloved image by becoming it himself. Don Jaime as a lover is here as steadfast, as tragic as Heathcliff plundering

Cathy's tomb in *Cumbres borrascosas*'.

5. On this aspect of the film see, in particular, Robert Havard, 'Luis Buñuel: Objects and Phantoms. The Montage of *Viridiana*', in *Luis Buñuel: A Symposium*, Leeds: Trinity and All Saints' College, 1983, pp. 59–85.

6. Raymond Durgnat, *op. cit.*, pp. 121–22, sees Jorge as infinitely inferior to his father, praising the latter for his romantic fidelity-after-death. David Robinson, 'Luis Buñuel and *Viridiana*', in *The World of Luis Buñuel*, p. 240, observes: 'If there is a hero at all, it is Jorge, who lives positively and (as a good surrealist) according to the dictates of desire. . .'

7. We should bear in mind that Bosch's famous picture hangs in the Prado in Madrid, and that Buñuel was a student at the famous Residencia de Estudiantes from 1917 to 1924. Bosch was, in any case, a painter greatly admired by the Spanish surrealists.

8. Francisco Aranda, *Luis Buñuel*, p. 180.

9. Emilio G. Riera, '*Viridiana*', in *The World of Luis Buñuel*, pp. 220–21, observes: . . . 'Buñuel does not group the beggars in an arrangement similar to the figures in Da Vinci's "Last Supper" in order to belittle Christ and his apostles by comparing them to some drunkards. What he is doing in this instance is reducing representation of the divine to the human scale. . .'

10. Quoted by Victor Casaus, '*Las Hurdes: Land Without Bread*', in *The World of Luis Buñuel*, p. 184.

11. Particularly apt here is David Robinson's observation, 'Luis Buñuel and *Viridiana*', p. 243, that 'Buñuel seems to have the ability to put pictures on the screen with the accuracy and certainty of a good paperhanger sticking up paper'.

The Exterminating Angel

The Exterminating Angel (*El Angel Exterminador*) received its première in Mexico on May 8, 1962, less than
a year after *Viridiana*, and was also shown at the Cannes
Film Festival. Reaction at Cannes was in general cool
and to some extent puzzled, although the International
Federation of Film Critics (FIPRESCI) awarded the film
its own prize. Subsequently, many critics have come to
regard *The Exterminating Angel* one of Buñuel's truly
great and memorable films, and it is certainly true to
say that its subject matter lies at the very heart of his
work for the cinema. In his second film, *L'Age d'or* in
1930, Buñuel had placed the bourgeoisie under the
microscope, notably in the extended central sequence
where the Marquis of X entertains his guests in his
luxurious villa near Rome. The one-time student of
insects had examined with the same fascination the
behaviour of well-to-do human beings and, in particular, their highly ritualized way of life: their immaculate
dress, their gestures and conversation, their self-con-
tained isolation from the problems of the world at
large. What he went on to do in *The Exterminating Angel*
was, as Raymond Durgnat has noted, make that earlier
drawing room sequence the setting for the entire film.[1]

Buñuel's preoccupation with the bourgeoisie was
part of his socialist and surrealist attitudes, both of
which were, of course, rooted in the notion of revolution. His statements regarding his own position in

relation to those who have money and power have
been many and consistent:

> Morality — middle-class morality, that is — is for
> me immoral. One must fight it. It is a morality
> founded on our most unjust institutions — reli-
> gion, fatherland, family culture — everything that
> people call the pillars of society.[2]

And again:

> The thought that continues guiding me today is
> the same that guided me at the age of twenty-five.
> It is an idea of Engels. The artist describes authen-
> tic social relations with the object of destroying the
> conventional ideal of the bourgeois world and
> compelling the public to doubt the perennial exist-
> ence of the established order . . .[3]

The exposure of bourgeois values is central to almost
all of Buñuel's films; a concern which links *L'Age d'or* to
The Exterminating Angel and this to *Belle de Jour* and *The
Discreet Charm of the Bourgeoisie*. There is one aspect of
bourgeois life that has become a central preoccupation
of Spanish literature and culture from Cervantes to
Galdós: the relationship between appearance and the
reality that underlies it. In Calderón's religious play,
God, the Only Good Fortune, the character Beauty falls
into a pit and, rescued by her companions, emerges as
a skeleton. In Goya's famous portrait of the Royal
Family, the finery of the King and Queen seems to
highlight rather than conceal their foolishness.

In order to explore reality and appearance, Buñuel
did more than place the characters of *The Exterminating
Angel* in an elegant house — he marooned them there.

As long ago as 1952, he had entertained the idea of making a film called *The Castaways*, based on a short story by José Bergamín, and by 1957 the project appeared to be even more certain, the title now expanded to *The Castaways of Providence Street (Los náufragos de la calle Providencia)*. In addition, Buñuel was by 1957 planning a film of William Golding's *Lord of the Flies*, in which a group of boys, cast away on an island, begin eventually to vent their feelings of frustration and desperation on each other. Neither of these films was actually made, although *The Exterminating Angel* is a distillation of both of them. The image of the bourgeoisie, separated from their fellow men, like Robinson Crusoe on an island which is, in fact, an elegant house, was one which clearly fascinated Buñuel.[4] Moreover, the disquieting nature of reality is presented not only to us, the audience of the film, but to the bourgeois characters of the film itself. They are obliged to observe their own natures, the emptiness and superficiality of the rites and rituals with which they surround themselves, their precarious hold on things, and the dark, frightening and often shameful world of their own, uncontrollable subconscious. Buñuel delights in shaking the bourgeoisie to its very foundations, forcing it to look into the fearful mirror of its own nightmares, as he would do again, with a lighter touch, in *The Discreet Charm of the Bourgeoisie* ten years later.

The opening sequences are intended to suggest two aspects of bourgeois appearance: firstly, superficial elegance; secondly, the importance of ritual. As the titles fade, a shot of an elegant suburban street — Providence Street — becomes that of the imposing, wrought-iron gates of a large house. This in turn is replaced by a shot of a splendid drawing room with fine, symmetrically arranged chairs, great china vases, heavy curtains and a glittering chandelier. This image of wealth and elegance is then developed further as the camera follows one of the household servants into the dining room where the long table is beautifully arranged with fine china, silverware, glasses and fruit bowls. Expensive pictures, statues and furniture adorn the rest of the room. The setting is one which is repeated from one Buñuel film to another (*L'Age d'or*, *Viridiana*, *Belle de Jour*, *The Discreet Charm of the Bourgeoisie*), the camera picking out with clarity and precision the array of beautiful and expensive objects which decorate the landscape of bourgeois life. And when the characters themselves appear, returning from an evening at the opera, they match, of course, the splendour of the house, the men decked out in dinner jackets, the women in evening gowns and expensive jewelry. As the group enters the hall of the great house with its interior balcony, marble stairway and magnificent chandelier, the image is complete, the façade of bourgeois elegance presented in all its grandiose and glittering detail.

The theme of ritual is emphasized through two striking repetitions. The arrival of the host, Nobile, and his guests is repeated almost immediately in an identical shot. Immediately afterwards Nobile rises to propose a toast to Silvia, an opera singer, sits down, then rises to propose the same toast again. Repetitions of this kind occur some twenty times in the course of the film, confusing the critics and allowing Buñuel to confuse them even more by saying that, had he left them out, the film would have been much shorter.[5] The explanation is more straightforward, for he has also said that repetition plays a part in all our lives: we get up each morning, brush our teeth, eat our breakfast, go to work, come back home and go to bed. But while this is so for all of us, it is more so for the bourgeoisie, whose lives consist of repetition raised to the level of ritual and rite: eating, drinking, attending the theatre. At the beginning of the film cars draw up outside the house in an almost processional manner, exactly as they do in *L'Age d'or*. These people are not simply returning from the theatre, they are themselves theatrical; their lives a true performance. The point is made particularly well in *The Discreet Charm of the Bourgeoisie* when the bourgeois group, believing they are in a restaurant, find themselves on stage, observed by a theatre audience and served cardboard chickens.

If bourgeois appearance is one of its characteristics, others are complacency and resilience, and *The Exterminating Angel* is not the only film in which Buñuel puts both to the test. From the outset the subversion of bourgeois plans is initiated by the servants' sudden departure for quite irrational reasons, the ordered nature of bourgeois life being thrown into confusion by it. Secondly, the conversation of the guests, characteristically elegant, is from time to time distinguished by strange lapses and aberrations. Alicia, for example, in conversation with Nobile, refers indiscreetly to her ageing husband's sexual energy:

> Well, after the concert he even tried to . . . I've nothing to complain about; I even have to restrain him.

Nobile, ever the polite host, replies that her husband may have her if he wishes at any moment:

> Let him sleep; he may try again here.

Similarly, Raul's inquiry about the progress of Leonora's cancer draws from the doctor the observation that in three months' time she will be completely bald. On the one hand, the shape and pattern of the dialogue are highly polished, retaining all its formal elegance. On the other, it is full of incongruities, unintentional errors, inappropriate responses, plain crudities. But no one really notices, other, that is, than the cinema audience. In *L'Age d'or* the Marquis talks to his guests, oblivious to the flies crawling on his face, while no one in the drawing room pays the slightest attention to the sudden appearance of a horse-drawn cart full of drunks. Buñuel mocks the bourgeoisie, pointing to its self-absorption and complacency, but is well aware that this is its very strength. From time to time the elegant image may well be disturbed or put out of joint, by social or political conflict, by left-wing terrorists, by fleeing servants, even by inner tensions, but in the end it remains intact.

This said, the film slowly begins to strip away the mask and to probe beneath the surface.[6] The guests discover they cannot leave the drawing room and are forced to spend the night there. Because of the heat, some of the men remove their jackets, some lie on the floor, others in chairs. The elegant image begins to break down into disarray as good manners yield to necessity. There are other, more disturbing signs. The following morning, having spent the night sleeping next to her brother, Juana is strangely affectionate towards him, attracted by his untidiness. Eduardo, Beatrice's lover, considers her dishevelment to be much more interesting than her normal state. And Ana expresses the view that this new experience is a welcome change from day-to-day routine.

Clearly, there are darker corners to the bourgeois mind than we, or they, suspected; untapped and unexplored areas of the subconscious buried beneath the thick layers of social, moral, educational and religious indoctrination. To this extent *The Exterminating Angel* is a truly surrealist film, in which the subconscious begins to rise to the surface, even if the characters in it are not exactly willing participants. Indeed, they make every effort to preserve their crumbling façade, clinging desperately to deeply ingrained social habits and graces. Lucía, the hostess, conscious of her social obligations, insists on providing breakfast, even if no milk has been delivered. Increasingly aware of their dishevelled appearance, the women attempt to comb and arrange their hair. The spectacle is often, of course, comic in its incongruity. Thus, Eduardo offers the thirsty Beatrice water from a flower-vase and, since he is a gentleman, adds a dash of lemon. Again, in the absence of a lavatory, the guests are obliged to avail themselves of a closet containing Chinese vases, which they enter and leave with characteristic discretion. The mask of gentility is still in place but secured only precariously.

Buñuel's ironic portrayal of social manners gradually becomes an exposure of deeper fears and anxieties, and the film's attention moves progressively from the external to the internal, outside to inside, appearance to inner reality. The structure of the film is therefore superbly logical, a natural progression in which nothing seems forced. The movement into the inner lives of the characters can be seen fairly early on when three of the women emerge from the closet, presumably after relieving themselves. Silvia observes that, when she looked down, she saw a precipice and a great torrent of water; Ana describes an eagle that flew close to her; and Rita a mass of dead leaves which flew in her face. The process is one of irrational fears released by a growing anxiety and sense of panic, intensified as time passes and pressures grow. In the course of the night Ana awakens, hot and thirsty, and is transfixed by the sight of a dead hand. In reality it is the hand of one of the guests, Mr Russell, who has died earlier of a heart-attack and whose body has been placed in a cupboard. Later in the film the hand appears again as Ana sleeps, sliding across the floor, climbing up her body and seizing her by the throat — a true beast with five fingers[7]; the exteriorization of deep-seated fears associated with sex and death. Buñuel's ability to expose in such a powerful plastic form the inner landscape of his characters' lives is one of the film's major attractions and achievements.

At given moments attention moves from the house to the world outside it, and the attempts being made by the army and the police to rescue the people inside. For Buñuel the police and the army are always the servants and instruments of the bourgeoisie and are, more often than not, portrayed in just as unfavourable a light as priests and bishops. In *L'Age d'or* the Buñuelian hero, Gaston Modot, is prevented from making love to his girl by two brutal policemen who drag him away and punch and kick him, and in *The Discreet Charm of the Bourgeoisie* the Chief of Police, no doubt reminiscent of the Parisian officer responsible for banning *L'Age d'or*, is shown torturing a young anarchist. Their presentation in *The Exterminating Angel* is somewhat different and, if anything, comic. In the first of the two episodes an officer reveals that a brigade of sappers attempted to enter the house but failed to do so, not, however, because they were driven back but because they lacked the resolve to enter. On the one hand there is something comic in the incongruity between the military scale and ambition of the exercise and the reason for such abject failure; and on the other, there is something delightfully witty in the fact that just as the bourgeoisie lacks the will to leave the house, so its henchmen, the police and the army, lack the resolve to enter it; the one cast in the image of the other.

In the second episode attention is centered on a professor and a priest, two more bastions of the ruling classes. The professor and the priest are distinguished by pomposity and hypocrisy respectively, the former convinced that he has the answer to free the entrapped people, the latter denouncing the child he had previously claimed would enter the house unimpeded. The picture that is constructed piece by piece is one that reveals both the moral emptiness of the bourgeoisie and its advocates and their pervasive influence.

Between these two episodes an extended sequence presents with great power and in minute detail the physical, emotional and moral degradation now taking place inside the house. In contrast to the order and neatness of the street outside, the initial shot reveals the butler, shirt-sleeved, hacking at the wall with an ornamental axe. The floor is covered with fallen plaster, the bricks of the wall exposed as he attempts to locate the water-pipes. Throughout the sequence the camera moves around the drawing room with precision, as it did at the film's beginning, but picking out devastation, not elegance, such as the large pile of rubbish accumulating near the doorway. And the wreckage of the room has its counterpart in the people who inhabit it. Blanca slumps in a chair, pulling at her hair. Beatrice is seated, eating paper. Francisco sits on the floor shaving, and Letitia stands in front of a mirror, squeezing blackheads on her nose. Above all, the suggestion of an organism slowly decaying and rotting is embodied (if that is the right word) in Mr Russell's corpse, the smell of which now fills the room, reminding the others forcibly of their own deterioration.

In conjunction with this visible wreckage, Buñuel charts too, as we have seen, the darker areas of the mind. Ana's vision of the dismembered hand was accompanied by a loud and regular ticking, and later by other dark and terrifying images, not necessarily related only to Ana, as the irrational takes control of the whole group.[8] By now these once elegant people are little different from the primitive characters who inhabit the slums of Mexico City in Buñuel's *The Young and the Damned (Los olvidados)*. There is also a clear link between Pedro's dream of the piece of raw, bleeding meat in the earlier film and Ana's vision of the crawling hand.

The conclusion of the sequence relates human beings to the world of animals, specifically sheep and a bear. Both have been briefly introduced earlier as part of a practical joke which the hosts intended to play on their guests. Now, however, the animals are seen in the house, the sight and sound of the bear on the upstairs landing a particular source of consternation. Significantly, it is not the bear which falls on the sheep as they make their way to the drawing room but ravenous human beings. As they do so, the camera moves upwards to pick out in close-up a glittering chandelier and, to the right of it, the bannister where the bear can be heard growling; bourgeois elegance and animal ferocity side by side.

A second extended sequence develops with even greater power the implications of the previous scene. The drawing room is now a wreck, reminiscent of some derelict city site where down-and-outs huddle around a fire. Sophisticated conversation has become the constant coughing of smoke-filled throats, objects of adornment and culture are now only things to keep the fire going. Attempts, however, are still being made even now to keep up appearance, for old habits die hard. In the midst of growing chaos Alicia cuts her toenails and Letitia puts her lipstick on. There is even talk of organizing a rota system to keep the place clean, but these are things which seem to suggest how blind these people are to what they have become. On a spit over the blazing fire a lamb is being roasted while another, tied to the elegant white grand piano, waits to be slaughtered. We are reminded of the beggar's feast in *Viridiana* and of their cry when left to themselves:

> We'll have ourselves a couple of lambs.
> We'll have them roasted.

The wreckage of the room is, if anything, even greater than the shambles left by the beggars. Moreover, there is little to separate the behaviour of its occupants either from the beggars or the animals as their hostility towards each other grows. The point is made clearly when Francisco attempts to push Leandro towards the roaming bear and a fight ensues in which the two men and Juana roll and struggle to the floor, the tangle of bodies, blows and shouts reminiscent of a dog-fight.

The inner lives of the characters is also more disturbed than before. In a wonderfully haunting and poetic sequence, voices cry out in the darkness: not the real voices of the characters but those inside their heads as they lie sleeping. There are frightening visions too, dissolving into each other: a shot of clouds with a close-up of Raul superimposed, evoking the tumult of his mind; a close-up of Letitia's face against a background of icy, snow-covered peaks; the Pope on top of the mountains; a saw cutting through a tree, which becomes a saw cutting through a hand; the saw slicing through a woman's forehead. This cinematically brilliant and inventive sequence, as powerful as any in Buñuel's work, is the true climax of the film, the moment in which all pretence has been stripped away to reveal the seething whirlpool of fear and anxiety. What emerges finally, therefore, is not so much the inhuman but the human face of the bourgeoisie — as human and as agonized as that of Robinson Crusoe, isolated on his desert island.

Their release from imprisonment is as sudden as it is revealing. In the course of a final desperate effort to save themselves, including Nobile's offer to sacrifice himself, the guests accidentally find themselves standing or sitting in exactly the same positions as those they had occupied on arrival at the house. As a consequence, they are suddenly and inexplicably free, and Letitia leads them in triumph to the safety of the outside world. In reality, the 'release' is full of irony. In the first place, it is clear that Nobile and his friends have not succeeded in saving themselves through any determined effort of their own. Throughout their incarceration they have made no conscious effort to escape and by reacting passively to their situation, they exemplify a typical bourgeois acceptance of things, an inertia which by definition excludes initiative and action.

The second irony is that their release is in fact an illusion. Some time later the same group of friends is seen in a church which is full of worshippers.[9] As the service ends, three priests attempt to leave by the vestry door but stop before it, baffled, while the rest of the congregation, attempting to leave by the front door, is also thwarted in its efforts to go out. Outside, meanwhile, a demonstration is taking place and the police are seen firing into the crowd. And finally a flock of sheep moves towards the cathedral door and begins to enter. In this last sequence one form of imprisonment has, of course, replaced another, for bourgeois life is as much the victim of religious and moral indoctrination as of its own paralyzing rituals. As far as the demonstration is concerned, it represents the threat to the bourgeoisie that is to be found in many Buñuel films: the left-wing terrorists who burst into the bourgeois house in *The Discreet Charm of the Bourgeoisie*, the terrorist bombs which explode in the street in *That Obscure Object of Desire*. The police, on the other hand, are the agents of the bourgeoisie's protection, linked in this respect to the Church. But above all the bourgeoisie survives and overcomes all obstacles as a consequence of its own sponge-like smugness and complacency which absorbs all dangers.[10] While revolutions may spread confusion, the bourgeoisie sits quietly at home, perhaps shaken, maybe stirred, but ready to emerge when things have settled down again.[11] It is perfectly conceivable that a bourgeois audience, watching *The Exterminating Angel*, would fail to recognize itself as the target of attack or, even if it did, would not treat it seriously. On the other hand, such a reaction is in itself a comment on and proof of the enormous accuracy with which Buñuel has portrayed the bourgeoisie.

Notes

1. Raymond Durgnat, *Luis Buñuel*, p. 136.

2. See Donald Richie, 'The Moral Code of Luis Buñuel', *The World of Luis Buñuel*, p. 111.

3. See Victor Casaus, *'Las Hurdes: Land Without Bread'*, *The World of Luis Buñuel*, p. 184.

4. Buñuel had made *Robinson Crusoe* ten years earlier, in 1952.

5. Buñuel had arranged for his son to tell the critics this. See 'A letter on The Exterminating Angel', *The World of Luis Buñuel*, p. 255.

6. See Michel Estève, '*The Exterminating Angel*: No Exit From the Human Condition', *The World of Luis Buñuel*, pp. 247–48: 'As the hours pass and day follows night in a rigorous implacable monotony, the masks fall, one by one, reduced to ashes in the fire of truth . . .'

7. In 1945 Buñuel, then in Hollywood, was involved indirectly in the making of Warner Brothers' horror film, *The Beast with Five Fingers*. Its director, Robert Florey, had asked Buñuel for his ideas on the dream sequence, but in the finished film only the episode of the hand remained. The idea of the dismembered hand goes back to Buñuel's very first film, *Un Chien andalou*.

8. See Francisco Aranda, *Luis Buñuel*, p. 210: 'In its language *El ángel exterminador* still remains the most distinctly and completely Surrealist film since *L'Age d'or*, and, in the writer's opinion, is second only to that film in Buñuel's whole *oeuvre*'.

9. Michel Estève, '*The Exterminating Angel* . . .', p. 249, notes; 'The guests leave the salon at last, but they can only understand the Te Deum as a new call to the old social structure, and they quickly don the masks of respectability and go on as before . . .'

10. The same is true of the bourgeois family in *Diary of a Chambermaid*, for its members shut their eyes to the disturbing events which are occurring in the world outside.

11. It is not only the bourgeoisie which survives — so do its allies, the police, the army, the Church. In *L'Age d'or* the skeletons of the bishops in the rocks mark not an end but a new beginning as they are honoured and replaced by priests, newly arrived on the island. And with the priests come representatives of the forces of law and order — as it were, the new Holy Trinity.

Tristana

Although it had been Buñuel's intention to make *Tristana* in 1962 after the completion of *The Exterminating Angel*, it was not in fact made until 1969. The delay was ostensibly caused by the intervention of the Spanish censorship on the grounds that the script's references to duelling contravened the regulations, but the real reason probably lay in the authorities' desire to take revenge for the scandal caused by *Viridiana*. At all events, Buñuel managed to make several films in the intervening seven years, of which *Diary of a Chambermaid* and, in particular, *Belle de Jour* were highly successful, and by 1969 appeared to have lost interest in *Tristana*. Nevertheless, filming commenced in the autumn of that year, there were few complications, and shooting was completed in the remarkably quick time of two months. Critical reaction proved, predictably, to be rather varied. Pilar de Cuadra, for example, complained in a review in the *Diario de Barcelona* that Buñuel had made his character Tristana altogether too bitter and disillusioned in the film's final scenes, betraying in this respect his novelistic source.[1] In contrast, César Santos Fontenla, writing in the Spanish film magazine, *Nuestro Cine*, saw *Tristana* as one of Buñuel's very best films, while Louis Marcorelles in *Le Monde* regarded its attack on the bourgeoisie as one of the most powerful in the cinema for many years.[2] What is perfectly clear twenty or so years on is that both in terms of its cinematic imagery and its indictment of particular social values, *Tristana* is one of Buñuel's best films.

Unlike either *Viridiana* or *The Exterminating Angel*, *Tristana* is based on a work by one of Spain's most famous writers; Benito Pérez Galdós. The film is faithful to this novel of the same name in many respects. In the latter Tristana's guardian is Don Juan, whom Galdós portrayed as a generous and sympathetic 'gentleman' now fallen on more difficult times. Later Tristana becomes his mistress but abandons him in order to pursue an affair with a young painter, an episode to which Galdós devoted considerable attention. Eventually she returns to Don Juan, marries him and settles for a conventional, domestic role in which she happily makes puddings for the delighted old man.[3]

Buñuel's changes relate, as might be expected, to this rather sickly and sentimental ending. The affair with the painter, Horacio, ends in the film when Tristana develops a tumour of the leg and, believing she is dying, returns to her uncle's house. The leg is amputated and she recovers but is subsequently filled with bitterness towards him for the way in which he has taken advantage of her in previous years and for the obvious pleasure he now takes in receiving her back, clearly hoping to turn her disability to his own advantage. Far from accepting the situation as the Galdós heroine does, Buñuel's Tristana exploits it. She marries Don Lope but proceeds to torment him, dismissing his attentions and leading an independent life. Don Lope's attitude towards women is embodied in the Spanish proverb which he quotes at one point: 'The honourable woman breaks her leg and stays at home'. It is this traditional repression which Tristana rebels against and which therefore makes this film, in its exploration of the theme of female liberty, so modern.

Buñuel's change of location from Madrid to Toledo is highly significant. Firstly, Toledo, a provincial city, suggests much better than Madrid a world enclosed by tradition. In order to suggest enclosure, Buñuel concentrated, firstly, on evoking the physical character of the place. When, for example, Don Lope directs a policeman down the wrong street, or when Tristana and Saturna take a stroll, we form an immediate impression of Toledo's narrow and often winding streets. On either side, moreover, the walls of buildings are high, creating a feeling of confinement and containment. The idea is suggested too by the episode in which the young and innocent Tristana and the two boys climb the narrow, twisting steps to the cathedral bell-tower. On several occasions the formal structures of the city's architecture are also emphasized — churches, convents, the regular arrangement of stone columns and pillars, as in the main square. Narrowness, enclosure and formality are the predominant physical characteristics carefully picked out by the camera. In terms of colour, drabness and dullness are much to the fore, especially the grey of stonework, but the muted effect is deliberate and precisely calculated. Toledo has all the greyness of a Spain imprisoned in the past. Coming back to it after an absence of many years, Buñuel observed: 'I don't like Toledo: it is old and stinks of piss'.[4]

The importance of tradition in the form of religion is suggested in the opening shot in which, as the titles roll, the cathedral is seen to dominate the city spread below it, and the only sound to be heard is that of the bells, monotonously tolling. The sense of lifelessness and joylessness, echoed in the drab sepia colour of the buildings, points already to the mounting, stifling, deadening effect of tradition and convention, a theme which is subsequently developed in a number of suggestive shots. When Tristana climbs to the cathedral bell-tower, the great bell is shown in close-up, its massive bulk filling the screen, thereby suggesting the weight and authority of the Church itself. When Tristana then steps inside the bell, she is literally enclosed by it, a visual image of the way in which the teachings and attitudes of the Church dominate and inhibit the lives of ordinary people.[5] Later, Tristana visits a church with Don Lope and the statue of an archbishop is seen in close-up, the camera picking out initially the crossed hands and the expression of piety and devotion. This is the traditional face of religion — compassionate and good at heart — but in the whitish marble, as in some of the suggestions of whiteness in *Viridiana*, there is also a coldness and hardness which point to the Church's lack of warmth and flexibility. Furthermore, the statue is part of a tomb, which inevitably carries with it associations of lifelessness and death, in complete contrast to the beauty and freshness of Tristana herself as she gazes at the statue's face.[6] Step by step Buñuel constructs a picture of the inescapable presence of the Church in Catholic Spain, and it is not without significance that Don Lope himself, self-confessed enemy of the Church, should by the end of the film spend his evenings in the company of priests, the lamp over the table evoking in its shape the cathedral bell. The visual signposts of the film point in the same direction.

The importance of social conformity is also revealed, as in *The Exterminating Angel*, in relation to dress. In an early sequence Don Lope is seen in the street, impeccably dressed in dark-blue suit, grey hat worn at a jaunty angle, handkerchief neatly placed in top pocket, gloves, and carrying a walking-stick. As he approaches, we are perhaps reminded at once of another character who walked through the streets of Toledo bent on making an impression: the '*hidalgo*' or gentleman in the six-teenth-century picaresque novel, *Lazarillo de Tormes*, whose entire life is geared to the importance of image, appearance and reputation.[7] Just as this gentleman — fallen, like Don Lope, on hard times — is portrayed in his house engaged in the daily ritual of washing his hands, dressing, girding his sword and so on, so in a later sequence Don Lope stands in front of his mirror, trimming and dying his beard. He is, in effect, the puppet of that Spanish conformity revealed in the ritual of the evening '*paseo*' or public promenade. And he is echoed in this respect by Tristana's lover Horacio who, having appeared initially as a bohemian artist, ends up as an even greater bourgeois than Don Lope himself. In the opening sequence of the film Tristana and Don Lope's servant, Saturna, are seen to be dressed in the traditional black of mourning, for Tristana's mother has recently died. What is particularly striking here is the way in which her freshness and beauty are encased and imprisoned by her clothes no less than, at the beginning of *Viridiana*, Viridiana's youthful good looks are imprisoned in her habit. On a purely visual level, then, the theme of the repressive and constricting nature of conventional social attitudes and beliefs is powerfully stated.

It is developed on another level in relation to Don Lope's views on the world and, in particular, on women. In many respects, he appears to be the embodiment of liberal and even anti-authoritarian behaviour, exem-plified in his sending a policeman in pursuit of a thief down the wrong street, his constant denigration of religion, and his often outrageous views on love:

. . . Passion must be free. It is the natural law.

No chains, no signatures, no blessings.

In other ways, however, Don Lope could not be more conservative.[8] When Tristana kneels to wipe away the polish she has spilled, Don Lope claims it is the servant's job. When Tristana kneels to put his slippers on his feet, he makes no objection. For him women have their roles within a household hierarchy in which men are supreme and to be served. His belief that a woman's place is in the home, so graphically illustrated by the proverb quoted previously, is not essentially different from the attitudes of fathers, guardians and husbands who fill the pages of seventeenth-century Spanish literature. And so it is that initially Tristana, rather like the wife in Cervantes's short-story, 'The Jealous Extremaduran', is allowed out of the house only to go to church. This sense of propriety hides a double standard: Don Lope's concern with protecting his niece from the wicked ways of the world does not prevent him from exploiting her sexually within the confines of the house. Significantly, he takes her into his bedroom after she has finished ironing, exploiting her in both ways. She is thus his slave and he her jailor in a society which, as Buñuel well knew, was largely distinguished by its deeply ingrained traditionalism.

The Spain in which the film is set is not, however, the Spain of Galdós's novel. As well as moving the story from Madrid to Toledo, Buñuel also set it in the twentieth, not the nineteenth century, and specifically in the years preceding the outbreak of the Spanish Civil War. These were, of course, the years of the Second Spanish Republic when, for a while, the ideals of freedom burned brightly and hopes for a new Spain, liberated from the shackles of the past, appeared to be more than empty dreams. In the end it was not to be, and in the film there are examples of the increasing violence that marked the period immediately before the War. At one point in the film a group of young men are pursued by the police with drawn swords; the Civil Guard on horse-back confront a line of angry and gesticulating men; and a group of people come running down a street chased by the police. In other films, as has been pointed out, the bourgeoisie is frequently set in the context of bomb-ings, terrorist attacks and social disturbance. *Tristana*, in contrast, evokes a period of freedom embodied by the Second Republic which is about to be swept away by a reassertion of traditional, conservative and au-thoritarian values. Buñuel's *Tristana* has echoes of Lorca's *The House of Bernada Alba*, written in 1936, embodying the struggle for freedom in a young woman and depict-ing Spain on the edge of bitter conflict.[9]

Tristana's experience is, like Viridiana's, a rite of passage, but over a longer period and with even harsher consequences. In this respect the early part of the film suggests quite beautifully her youth, innocence and inexperience, expressed in shot after shot of her flaw-less, luminous face, her wide-eyed expression and her pigtails. But already there are moments which point to her awakening sexuality, to a girl poised on the brink of womanhood, with all the curiosity, embarrassment, doubt, uncertainty and fear that this implies. Very revealing in this respect is the sequence in which, accompanied by Saturno and another boy, she climbs to the belltower of the cathedral. As they go up the narrow stairs, Tristana leading the way, Saturno looks up her skirt, much to her indignation. In the belltower itself she is drawn to touch the bellclapper, whose phallic shape is very evident. Just as in *Viridiana* Buñuel so brilliantly used particular objects to reveal the inner life of the characters, so here in a single yet highly

suggestive shot Tristana's growing sexual awareness is
vividly suggested. But this is capped when suddenly,
looking across at another bell, she sees the clapper
transformed into the severed head of her uncle, Don
Lope. The horror written all over her face is then repeated when, in the very next shot, she awakens from a
dream of the same vision. In short, the presence of Don
Lope haunts her, awake or asleep, her sexual curiosity
interwoven with fears of male domination. And since
Don Lope's head has been cut from his body, her fears
contain perhaps a longing for his death or castration. At
all events, the suggestions of domination, castration
and crippling are deeply prophetic both in relation to
Don Lope and to Tristana herself.[10]

In matters of love and sexual morality, Don Lope's
double-edged views are crucial in shaping the young
Tristana's thinking. Observing a married couple, he
comments on their bored and bovine expressions and
advises Tristana not to marry. If the young Tristana is,
then, a *tabula rasa*, it is not surprising that, in relation to
the question of a woman's place in the world, Don
Lope's statements should make their mark. At one
point in the film she asks him if a woman cannot be free
and respectable at the same time. Elsewhere she poses
a question which he fails to understand: 'Which of
these pillars do you like most?' His reply — 'They are
all the same' — ignores or fails to grasp the point of
Tristana's question which is really about the freedom to
choose.

Her preoccupation with this issue is revealed by two
other incidents: firstly when, out for a walk with Saturna,
she wonders which of two streets they should take; and
secondly when, as she sits at the table, she wonders
which of two peas she should eat first. On a different
and more serious level the question of choice is one

which will inevitably preoccupy Tristana in matters of men, love and sex, and in such areas the act of choosing, as well as its consequences, are much more momentous than in relation to streets or peas. In addition, her freedom of choice, like that of any individual, must at least consider or take into account the views of the individuals and the society with which she comes into daily contact.

The central section of the film develops all these implications. Having taken Tristana as his mistress, Don Lope has practiced what he preaches, but has denied her the freedom which, ironically, he has taught her to cherish. She, perfectly aware of the inconsistencies in his behaviour, exercises her own freedom of choice by taking the young painter, Horacio, as her lover. For Tristana, however, it is already a freedom for which she struggles at no small cost. Don Lope may advocate free love, but when his mistress gives herself to someone else his liberal principles soon become conventional morality:

> Don't forget that I am responsible for you in two more ways: I am your father and your husband.

Horacio, younger, bohemian and less conventional than Don Lope, is a modern man. Nevertheless, it is he who expresses his belief in marriage and asks Tristana to marry him, but she refuses. When we see him visiting Don Lope's house to arrange Tristana's return, it is not the bohemian image which strikes us but that of middle-class respectability as he appears in long black overcoat and matching black hat. Horacio's bohemian fling is both superficial and temporary. Tristana, rejecting Don Lope's double standards, finds them echoed in Horacio. The men in the film fail to deliver what they promise, merely proving that they too are ultimately the prisoners of the society in which they live.

It is left to Tristana to fight her corner. Throughout the middle section of the film it is she who is the true rebel, defying Don Lope, visiting Horacio in his studio, coming home late and throwing Don Lope's slippers into the rubbish-bin. She presents the old man with his own arguments:

> Am I not free? I only have to answer to myself. Don't you see I'm only taking your advice?

When she leaves him for Horacio, she reminds the latter that she is free to do so:

> I know I'm not respectable . . . but I'm free to love you.

But if she is free to love him, she is still not freed from the moral and social attitudes which are part of her upbringing. There is a revealing moment when, having kissed her in the street, Horacio is berated by a passer-by and Tristana begs him not to continue the argument:

> Horacio, don't place me in an awkward position! Let's go home!

To this extent Tristana's struggle for freedom is as circumscribed by deeply ingrained beliefs as are Don Lope and Horacio. However, she is soon trapped in another way. During the affair with Horacio she develops a tumour of the leg, as a consequence of which she returns to Don Lope's house where her leg is eventually amputated. For him her return is a triumph: the recovery of an errant mistress who now has nowhere else to go and whose physical disability makes her an unlikely target for other men. For Tristana these events are a savage blow, depriving her of the independence she had struggled to obtain. The image of Tristana in a wheelchair, guided by Don Lope, or hobbling within the confines of her bedroom, speaks volumes.

Considered from one point of view, the Tristana of the latter part of the film is a figure of considerable heroism. When she has learned to walk again with an artificial leg, her peculiar gait, jerky and full of effort, suggests a struggling but defiant human being. When she bangs her stick on the floor, like Lorca's Bernarda Alba, as a signal for Don Lope to push her wheelchair, she asserts her unmistakable authority. And in a scene on the balcony she exercises her sexual power when, with Saturno watching from below, she opens her dressing-gown to allow him to feast his eyes on her naked body. It is the relationship of worshipper and worshipped, the dominant Tristana inspiring awe in the gawping Saturno no less than the figure of the Virgin in Spanish churches looks down from on high upon the congregation. Indeed, the point is made when the shot of Tristana becomes that of the Virgin in the church where Tristana's marriage to Don Lope is taking place. In the balcony scene the camera emphasizes height — Tristana above, Saturno below — and thus her domination of the young man, which will also now become her domination of Don Lope.[11] After the wedding, her very first act is to refuse to sleep with Don Lope, dismissing him as though he were a child. She is a defiant, assertive and heroic spirit, and in that sense gloriously free.

At the same time there is an essential difference. While Tristana's twisted walk evokes effort and defiance, it is also the walk of someone severely crippled and damaged, and her physical disability is soon revealed to be a metaphor for damage of another kind. In one sense Tristana's experience has led to growth and resilience, in another to coldness and harshness. The living embodiment of 'the honourable woman' who breaks her leg and stays at home, she is also more than that. The traditional ethos pictures a woman whose emotional and physical horizons are limited. Tristana, by contrast, has broken her bonds, but in so doing she has become incapacitated in another way, unable to feel warmth and compassion for other people. The latter part of the film emphasizes very strongly both her harshness and her coldness.

A sequence towards the end of the film reveals Don Lope at home in the company of priests. They are drinking chocolate and chatting in a friendly fashion while, outside the room, Tristana paces the corridor, her crutches creating a harsh and uncomfortable dragging sound. It is a sound which encapsulates the harshness which is now one of Tristana's distinguishing features. As for her coldness, it emerges in a variety of ways during the last third of the film. In the early scenes Tristana's pale and flawless face, frequently shown in close-up, expressed her youthful innocence. In the balcony scene that beauty has become a cold and cruel mask as she wields her sexual power over Saturno.[12] In a sense the whiteness of the face has something of the colour and quality of marble, bringing to mind the statue of the archbishop seen earlier in the film. At all events, the triumphant smile is a measure of the distance travelled by Tristana from the time when Saturno playfully looked up her skirt.[13]

The idea of coldness is reinforced in other ways. The film's concluding scenes take place in winter. Outside the house the snow is falling heavily, settling thickly on the ground. As Don Lope suffers a heart attack, Tristana opens the window on a bleak and barren scene; the only sound is that of an icy and merciless wind. The coldness of Nature presented by the open window, is also that of Tristana whose motive in letting in the cold air is merely to precipitate Don Lope's death. Beyond that, the open window reveals a desolate landscape that is a pointer to Tristana's future. In *Viridiana* the open window reveals the outside world from which Viridiana herself cannot escape and with which she must therefore come to terms. The perspective here is more pessimistic. Tristana has escaped from Don Lope's clutches and will now inherit his house and whatever money he has. She is still, of course, young, but who will want to marry a crippled woman, especially one as fiercely independent as we know her to be? Her future is more likely to be one of lonely widowhood, attended by Saturna and her deaf-mute son in an otherwise empty house.

The film's final sequence takes the form of a running flashback in which, as Tristana ensures that Don Lope is dead and closes the window, the things that have happened since her arrival at her uncle's house rush through her mind: her marriage to and rejection of him, her relationship with Saturno, her affair with Horacio, her seduction by Don Lope, her arrival as his ward. The sequence is one in which the sound of crashing waves and a howling wind create a sense of powerful turbulence appropriate to the trauma experienced by Tristana. Beyond that, it also creates a clear contrast between what Tristana is and what she was, and in particular a sense of innocence lost and freedom won at considerable cost. At the end of the flashback is the young, pale, beautiful girl, a blank page on which life is still to make its mark; at its beginning the older woman on whom its mark has been made, a woman driven by a narrow-minded society into a rebellion which ends in her victory, but a victory that is bitter and costly. *Viridiana* ends with a young woman's acceptance of the world for what it is. The one-time novice becomes the mistress of the pragmatic and unsentimental Jorge who will doubtless abandon her. In *Diary of a Chambermaid* a young woman, Célestine, marries Mauger, a one-time rebel who has since become a typical bourgeois, the kind of man Célestine detests. In all three films escape leads only to another imprisonment, illustrating that ultimately man is not free. Tristana's experience is a powerful example of that point of view.

Notes

1. *Diario de Barcelona*, 9 April, 1970.

2. *Nuestro cine*, 96, Madrid, April 1970, and *Le Monde*, Paris, May 1970, respectively.

3. Buñuel is said to have observed during shooting that *Tristana* contained forty per cent of Galdós's dialogue, though the film was essentially his. He was also of the opinion that *Tristana* was Galdós's worst novel.

4. Francisco Aranda, *Luis Buñuel* . . . p. 241.

5. The episode of the bell had been used by Buñuel previously in *El*, made in 1953, when he depicts an attempted strangling by the paranoiac Francisco, whose fixations are in large part attributable to his narrow religious upbringing.

6. The shot is, interestingly enough, the reverse of what

occurs in *Viridiana* where Viridiana is the recumbant figure as Don Jaime leans over her.

7. The influence on Buñuel of the literature of Spain's Golden Age, and of the nineteenth century, cannot be overemphasized. Clear echoes of it are to be found throughout the Spanish films: the picaresque novel in *Los olvidados*, *Don Quixote* in *Nazarín*; Galdós in *Nazarín* and *Tristana*; the mystics in *Viridiana*; and the Golden Age theatre, especially Calderón, in the honour-obsessed characters of many of Buñuel's films.

8. The quotation embodying Don Lope's inherent conservatism is perceptively discussed by Freddy Buache in *The Cinema of Luis Buñuel . . .*, pp. 177–78.

9. There are many similarities, of both a specific and a general nature, between *Tristana* and Lorca's play.

10. In relation to Buñuel's fascination with the revelation of his characters' unconscious mind, it is important to take into account his reading of the works of Freud in the 1920s and 1930s. He has stated that in 1921 he read Freud's *Psychoanalysis of Daily Life* in Spanish translation. Subsequently, between 1922 and 1934 the works of Freud were translated into Spanish by the Biblioteca Nueva.

11. On the importance of height see R.G. Havard, 'The Seventh Art of Luis Buñuel: *Tristana* and the Rites of Freedom', *Quinquereme*, 5, (1982), pp. 56–74.

12. Tristana here is not unlike one of those prostitutes who display themselves to passers-by in the windows of houses in various European cities.

13. After the amputation of Tristana's leg, Don Ambrosio, the priest, observes that 'there is something Satanic in that harshness of hers'. There are several occasions earlier in the film when Don Lope has been compared to the Devil, the implication being that Tristana has

acquired some of his characteristics. The process has been seen by one critic as a kind of vampirism, and there is no denying that the shot of Tristana's smiling but cold face is reminiscent of the portrayal of vampire figures in many commercial horror films. See Tom Hutchinson, *Horror and Fantasy in the Cinema*, London: Studio Vista, 1974, pp. 64–67.

The Hunt

By 1965, the year in which Saura made *The Hunt* (*La caza*), he had completed only two full-length films: *The Drifters* (*Los golfos*) in 1959, and *Lament for a Bandit* (*Llanto por un bandido*) in 1963. The former, as its title suggests, is about the lives of layabouts and criminals and implies that in Franco's Spain hope is denied to the young. In consequence, the censorship decided to clip Saura's wings by allowing the film only limited distribution. When, therefore, he made *Lament for a Bandit* four years later, he considered it prudent to comment more obliquely on the contemporary political situation, and took as his subject the life of the nineteenth-century Andalusian bandit, José María Hinojosa, popularly known as 'El Temperanillo'. As supporters of the liberal cause against the monarchists, the bandits are roughly equated with those Republican soldiers who, after the Civil War, lived like virtual outlaws, while the monarchists are earlier versions of Franco's fascists. Censored to some extent (interestingly enough, a scene in which Buñuel played the part of an executioner was cut) the commercial failure of the film was a great disappointment to its thirty-one year old director, but it was also a landmark in his career in that it taught him in which direction he should go as a film-maker.

This process was greatly facilitated too by the fact that for the shooting of *The Hunt* in 1965 Saura had as his producer Elías Querejeta, with whom he would build an artistic partnership that would continue for eleven more films and which had as its basis a particular policy. Briefly stated, this consisted of: a regular and highly talented crew; a single, often enclosed setting in or near Madrid; a smallish cast with at least one star; an anti-Francoist position which deliberately challenged the censorship; an emphasis on sex and violence which threw out a challenge to the notion of a changing, modernized Spain; and a documentary quality which frequently amounts to the fictionalization of contemporary problems.[1] *The Hunt* is a film in which many of these elements came together for the first time.

Originally called *The Rabbit Hunt* (the censorship insisted that the title be changed on the grounds that rabbits had sexual connotations), the film was shown for the first time in November 1966 for one week in five cinemas. Critical reaction proved to be very favourable. César Santos Fontenla considered *The Hunt* to be an essential film in the evolution of Spanish cinema, while Gutiérrez Aragón observed that 'there is one Spanish cinema before *The Hunt* and another one afterwards'.[2] Saura must have been pleased too by Buñuel's comment that, in its typically Spanish violence, it was the best film he had seen in the whole of the Spanish cinema.[3] Nevertheless, much to Saura's disappointment, *The Hunt* was not selected to be shown at Cannes, although compensation came subsequently when it was awarded the Silver Bear at the Berlin Film Festival and made a considerable impression at film festivals in New York, London and Acapulco.

The Hunt is the story of one day in the lives of three middle-aged, middle-class businessmen, Paco, Luis and José, and Paco's younger brother-in-law, Enrique, as they go rabbit-hunting in the countryside outside Madrid. Paco is a former driver of José who has now made his way in the world. In contrast, the business in which José and Luis are partners is in serious financial difficulties, and both men also have considerable personal problems: José is separated from his wife, has taken up with a young woman, and is plagued by a persistent stomach problem; Luis has been abandoned by his wife, has taken to drink, and constantly reads science fiction. The countryside in which the rabbit-hunt takes place is full of reminders of the Civil War, in which the three older men were involved, and, as the day advances and the sun beats down, tensions between them begin to rise. Paco rejects José's request for a substantial loan and offends him by offering him work instead. When Luis starts using a tailor's dummy for target-practice, José punches him in the face. Later, when the heat and alcohol have taken their effect, Paco is shooting at a fleeing rabbit when José blasts him full in the face. Luis, in turn, drives the Land Rover straight at José, who shoots Luis through the windscreen but fails to kill him. Struggling down from the vehicle, Luis shoots and kills José and then succumbs to his own wounds. Enrique, the only survivor, runs away from the terrible scene.

The film's opening titles roll over a sequence depicting ferrets in a cage. The style is that of a documentary and is strongly reminiscent of the opening sequence of Buñuel's *L'Age d'or* with its shots of scorpions. Just as in the earlier film the documentary opening becomes a study of the lives of human beings, so *The Hunt* begins with a sequence whose implications for the rest of the film are rich indeed. For ferrets are hunters, and they anticipate the human hunters who are soon to appear. In addition, ferrets are notoriously vicious and ferocious creatures, and the pair in the cage are kept in separate compartments to prevent them tearing each other apart.

In human terms this is precisely what Spaniards have already done to each other in the Civil War, and a pointer to the events of the film, in which the characters are literally caged animals. Franco's Spain therefore becomes, in a very real sense, a cage or prison in which men and women are prisoners not only of each other, but also of the past and the mark it has made upon them. The ominous implications of the opening sequence are reinforced by an insistent, jerky and increasingly loud musical accompaniment which recurs in a variety of forms throughout the rest of the film.[4]

The first twenty minutes or so of the film proper consist of, firstly, the arrival of Paco, Luis, José and Enrique at a roadside bar, and, secondly, their preparations for the hunt. From the very outset the use of landscape in the film is seen to be of key importance, the opening shot portraying a highway and a flat, bare, stark, desolate and sun-bleached countryside, its emptiness and harshness heightened in black and white. Slightly later, when the group leaves the bar to drive into the area where the hunt will take place, this effect is filled out. The sun beats down mercilessly on a place which is largely desert and full of stones, scrub, thistles and dust. As the roadside bar — the last outpost of civilization, as it were — is left behind, the landscape begins to acquire a timeless, universal quality, reminiscent of the poetry of Antonio Machado in which the Castilian heartland is at once a reminder of the glory that was Spain, as well as of the wretched place it has become. Indeed, this landscape is now linked specifically to other killings that took place there some thirty years previously. In reply to a question by Enrique, for example, Luis replies: 'Many people died here.' In a conversation with Paco, José observes, 'That time we were down below', specifically linking them to the events which occurred there previously. The linking of the present to the past or, to put it another way, the mark made by the past on the present, is something which is progressively suggested as the film unfolds and is one of its most important features.

The filming of the preparations for the rabbit-hunt brilliantly suggests the overlap of the past and the present.[5] A series of close-ups of guns being cleaned, prepared, loaded, cocked and aimed instantly bridges the passage of time. For a Spanish audience, many of whom would have been involved in those events of thirty or so years ago, the experience of being transported back in time, of having the ghosts of the past resurrected before their eyes, would have been particularly vivid, as well as in many cases painful. There is an especially telling moment when, through the telescopic sight of Enrique's rifle, the figure of a man is seen descending a hill, as if about to become the victim of a deadly bullet. When Enrique produces a Luger which belonged to his father, Luis observes: 'More than one died from one of those.'

The opposing forces in the Civil War are evoked here by Paco, José and Luis, all Francoist sympathizers who prospered after the War, and the gamekeeper, Juan, who lives in abject poverty in a broken-down house with his senile mother and his young niece, clearly representing the Republican losers. The three Francoists, and in particular Paco, embody attitudes which were wholly characteristic of the Right before and during the War and which continued to be evident during the dictatorship.[6] Above all, Paco is the very personification of Spanish 'machismo' or 'manliness', which asserts male superiority in most areas of life, including sexual and family relationships, and will not tolerate any deviation from the norm. His comment on rabbits —

'the weak have no place in life' — shocks the younger, impressionable Enrique, doubtless because it reveals a scant regard for human life as well. A little later, in a conversation about diseased rabbits, Paco expresses a profound distaste for any form of physical imperfection: 'I can't stand cripples. They make me shudder . . . I'd prefer to die rather than be lame.' In addition, Paco's attitude to women is typically condescending. It is significant that, apart from Juan's senile mother and his niece, who is little more than a child, the only women in the film are those displayed in the pages of a soft porn magazine. As Paco looks at them, Luis has been talking about the flesh-eating habits of piranhas, which Paco immediately and typically relates to the pictures of naked female bodies: 'What a time they would have with these!' This tasteless joke has the effect of exposing Paco and his like as the true predator, an exploiter of women in a male-dominated society where women are either wives, mothers or whores, at the disposal of men.[7] Later on, a female tailor's dummy will be used for target practice. Significantly, the part of Paco in *The Hunt* is played by Alfredo Mayo who during the 1940s had appeared in various 'approved' war films as a typical '*franquista*' hero and who is, therefore, used here as an extension of that role some twenty years later. But if Paco is the individual who appears to represent most strongly the Francoist philosophy, there are numerous occasions when Luis and José are seen to be kindred spirits.

If ferrets suggest ferocity, rabbits introduce the theme of disease, a notion central to this film. There is much talk, in particular, of myxomatosis and at one point a diseased rabbit is found in a trap. But the disease which affects the animals is a reflection of the ills which affect men. On a purely physical level Juan, the gamekeeper, suffers from a damaged leg, injured by a trap, while José suffers constantly from a stomach condition. The rabbit trap is, clearly, a metaphor for the larger trap in which the defeated Republicans find themselves, permanently damaged by the consequences of the War, living, like Juan, in poverty. José's stomach condition, on the other hand, seems to be caused to a large extent by the turmoil of his business affairs and his personal life, and he has his counterpart in Luis whose alcoholism will soon presumably trigger physical symptoms. The victors in the War are, then, damaged in a variety of ways. When the diseased rabbit is discovered, it leads Enrique to conclude: 'It wasn't like a rabbit, not even an animal. It was a monster.' These are words which might equally be applied to Paco and his like; the self-satisfied, intolerant, aggressive, unsympathetic macho-man, very much a monster in that he is totally lacking in more human qualities. If the Franco dictatorship sought to project the image of a Spain strong on moral values, family virtues and the like, the reality was that the country was affected by its own kind of myxomatosis.[8]

The depiction of the rabbit-hunt itself is full of extraordinary violence. From the outset the military parallel is carefully suggested as José instructs his companions in the tactics of the campaign, and Luis is led to observe: 'Look, this seems to be a military operation.' Indeed, as the men set out, advancing towards a hill, and the sound-track becomes an insistent kettle drum, this could well be an episode from the Civil War itself in which infantrymen, guns at the ready, scour the land ahead for any signs of movement. When the shooting begins the double image of past and present is constantly suggested. Close-ups of the hunter's faces, intense, excited and sweating, could equally be those of

Nationalist soldiers three decades earlier. When the
dog, Cuca, seizes and violently shakes an escaping
rabbit, its terrible squeals become in our imagination
the agonized screams of dying men. As rabbits are
blasted in full flight, their mutilated bodies rolling
down hillsides, the military implications of the sequence are underlined too. From the beginning, it is
accompanied by the insistent, war-like sounds of piano
and drums. As the sequence unfolds, the sound of
gunshots increases in frequency, underpinning the
music, building steadily towards a wild and frenetic
climax. And finally, when the hunt is over, the way in
which the hunters stand to be photographed, guns in
hand, triumphant, cannot fail to remind us of photographs we have all seen of soldiers at the Front.[9]

The accelerating rhythm of the hunt gives way to an
altogether quieter section of the film in which action
becomes conversation, and attitudes and tensions are
further revealed. But there is little in this film that is
irrelevant and two episodes here require detailed comment. The first concerns Paco and José who take a quiet
stroll and arrive at the entrance to a cave now blocked
by a padlocked door. José insists that Paco see his
'secret'. Unlocking the door, he leads Paco inside and
shows him, to his horror and disgust, a skeleton dressed
in rags. Earlier in the film José had made a comment
about the 'time we were down below'. This skeleton,
which has been José's secret, undoubtedly comes from
'that time'; in all probability the remains of a Republican soldier who, fleeing from the enemy, had hidden in
the cave and either succumbed to his wounds or starved
to death. For José and Paco, and for many other Spaniards, it is literally the skeleton in the cupboard; a guilty
memory of the horror and the crimes committed and
subsequently buried but which are always rising to

haunt them. Secondly, the shot of José and Paco inside the cave links them with the way in which ferrets are introduced into rabbit warrens and anticipates a particularly unpleasant and violent sequence later in the film.

The other episode which calls for comment occurs when Enrique and Luis visit a nearby village and watch a goat, suspended by a hook, being skinned. The camera focuses in close-up on the knife cutting the skin from the head and then on the slicing open of the abdomen. As they observe the process, Luis refers to Paco as someone who exploits others and in financial matters 'skins' them, thereby giving the moment a particular significance. This episode occurs, significantly, at the same time as Paco and José are looking at the skeleton in the cave and is therefore linked to that incident thematically. Indeed, in visual terms there is little difference between the skinned carcass of an animal and a human corpse. Looked at from this point of view, the episode becomes an image of the way in which, during the Civil War, Spaniards butchered each other, an image of man as both executioner and victim; a twentieth-century version of a theme graphically illustrated by Goya in his powerful series of etchings entitled 'The Disasters of War'.

Both episodes described above are important in the sense that they not only evoke the War but also suggest that there is no escape from it thirty years on. When Enrique and Luis have returned from the village and the four men eat their meal, José's reference to the fact that during the War men ate rats suggests that memories of the War are never far away. Indeed, the mark left by the War in terms of honing and sharpening whatever innate violence lies in the Spanish race is evident throughout the remainder of the film. As Paco tries to sleep, a story is being told on the radio of a girl being killed by dogs, its words repeated by Paco himself as sleep overtakes him. When the camera moves from Paco to José, it is unclear whether the voice we hear is that on the radio or the voice of his own conscience, perhaps resurrecting the past in which a woman pleads: 'Don't touch me!' At all events, awake or asleep, Paco, Luis and José are men for whom violence is never far away, be it in the form of hunting rabbits, the hostility of personal relationships or the turbulence of their inner lives. Prior to the rabbit hunt, Luis was seen crushing a beetle beneath his foot. Later, in another act of purely gratuitous cruelty, he pierces a beetle with a pin before placing it on the tailor's dummy in order to blast it to bits with a rifle. But his is not the only kind of violence. On another level, when José begs Paco to help him escape financial problems, Paco coldly turns him down — 'Friendship is one thing, money another' — and further offends him by offering to employ him. But José can hardly complain for, prior to this, he has himself refused to contribute towards the cost of the medicines which his gamekeeper, Juan, needs for his sick mother. There is, then, a closely interwoven network of harshness and violence of different kinds in which all these characters are trapped.

In conversation with Enrique, Luis observes at one point that everyone depends on someone else, while later, after he has slept, José remarks: 'We aren't living, locked up here.' Taken together the two statements point not only to the fact that these are men whose lives are inextricably interlocked by their past experience, but that the Spain in which they live is a prison from which there is no escape. It is not without significance that, as Luis blasts the beetle with the rifle and José attacks him physically in response to his wild behav-

iour, the ferrets are reintroduced. A shot of them being
carried in their cage by Juan immediately underlines
the notion of Spain as a prison inhabited by men dis-
posed to violence.

Enrique, in contrast, stands for the younger Spain,
the new generation. Unlike the three older men, he has
not been directly involved in the War and, as a result,
his role for much of the film is that of an observer, much
less detailed and developed than those of his three
companions.[10] It is fitting that he should ask about the
area in which they are hunting. His question, 'Did the
War take place here?' displays the curiosity of the
young to know more about their country's past. It is
revealing too that, in response to Paco's observation
that, 'The weak have no place in life,' he should react
with astonishment, for he has not been exposed to
those experiences which have helped shape the older
men. Their memories of the place in which they find
themselves are of the violence of the past, while Enrique's
are totally different: 'I have the impression of having
been here before. I like it. The heat, the scent of thyme
. . .' When Enrique dances with Juan's young niece to
the pop music on the radio, the image is one of a more
relaxed and uninhibited younger Spain, unencumbered
by the past. On the other hand, there are also signs that
they cannot escape it entirely. When Enrique is obliged
to look at a diseased rabbit, the horror of the moment
stays with him. In much the same way he cannot escape
the reality of the older, 'diseased' generation with their
hatreds and their prejudices. To a certain extent he is
influenced by them, for it is Enrique who blasts a rabbit
with a rifle as it emerges from its warren. And he
certainly cannot escape the violence unleashed in the
film's final scenes.

Before that violent conclusion, two episodes require

comment. The first involves a fire lit by Enrique. After a while Luis places the tailor's dummy on the fire and the flames begin to lick around it. Seen in close-up, the burning figure becomes an image of the horror and destruction of the War. Soon, however, the fire begins to spread and, as the men move through the smoke in a desperate attempt to put out the flames, the images remind us of newsreels we have seen of burning fields and villages in war zones throughout the world. Both before and after the fire Luis is reading a novel in which the end of the world is described: 'There was rain, wind, hail . . .' The whole sequence, therefore, evokes both the catastrophe which engulfed Spain and the mark it has left behind: a land scorched by its own violence, a land full of damaged people who have been through fire. For many it was indeed the end of the world.

The second episode concerns a ferret introduced into a rabbit-hole. The ferret is seen inside the tunnel, sniffing its way towards two frightened rabbits. One of them squeals pitifully as the ferret seizes it. Its companion emerges from the other end of the tunnel and is shot by Enrique. The first rabbit, having escaped from the ferret, also appears, the ferret in pursuit, and both are violently killed by Paco. The sequence is particularly rich in meaning. It is linked both visually and thematically with the earlier sequence of the cave in which José and Paco see the skeleton, and suggests, therefore, the ruthless hunting down of Republicans by Nationalists during the Civil War. But here both rabbit and ferret, victim and hunter, end up dead. The episode points to the fact that the victors of the War have themselves become the victims of the violence which they committed, and anticipates too the carnage which is about to occur amongst the victorious hunters.[11]

The tensions that have been evident from the outset are now irreconcilable. Paco's shooting of the ferret in the previous episode has been an act of sheer malice which José will not forgive and which, combined with Paco's refusal to help resolve his financial problems, drives him to the final act of violent revenge. Luis, moreover, will never forgive José for attacking him earlier and eagerly accepts the offer of a job from Paco which José has previously rejected. All three men are thus increasingly caught up in a web of mutual antagonism in which the hunters are finally the victims. As Paco kills a scurrying rabbit and turns away in triumph, José shoots him in the face. Luis, at the wheel of the Land Rover, drives it at José who shoots Luis through the windscreen but fails to kill him. As José attempts to escape, his gun empty, Luis fires at him and finally wounds him fatally before succumbing to his own wounds. The earlier, bloody sequence of the rabbit hunt is now one in which the hunters shoot each other, their own violence turned against themselves.

The last moments of the film show Enrique running away from the carnage, climbing a steep slope towards the top of a hill. As he does so, we see the sky and the sunlight touching his head. In one sense the sequence suggests optimism, the light after the darkness, the hope for the future that often follows tragedy. On the other hand, although Enrique leaves the carnage behind, it will have left its mark on him, no less than the aftermath of the Civil War itself left its mark on a generation of Spaniards. In 1965, ten years before the death of Franco and the end of the dictatorship, it was perhaps too much to hope that this mark would disappear.

Notes

1. For an informative account see John Hopwell, *Out of the Past: Spanish Cinema after Franco*, London: British Film Institute, 1986, pp. 71–72.

2. *Nuestro Cine*, no. 51, 1966, and A.M. Torres, 'Conversaciones con Manuel Gutiérrez Aragón', Madrid: Fundamentos, 1985, p. 28.

3. In number 63, *Nuestro Cine*.

4. Saura's 'realism' is never pure realism. He himself had been dissatisfied with the so-called realism of the Spanish novel of the 1950s and 1960s. The documentary beginning of *The Hunt* opens out, therefore, into a treatment of the subject which is constantly allusive and symbolic, in which things and objects are more than their surface meaning. See Agustín Sánchez Vidal, *El cine de Carlos Saura*, Zaragoza: Caja de Ahorros de la Inmaculada, 1988, p. 46.

5. John Hopewell, *Out of the Past* ..., p. 73, notes that Saura 'depersonalizes the hunters' cruelty in the gun-loading episode and the hunt sequence... Any of the hunters — and, as far as they typify a class, any Francoist — could be capable of such cruelty'.

6. See Virginia Higginbotham, *Spanish Film under Franco*, Austin: University of Texas Press, 1988, p. 80.

7. The attitudes here are little different from those of the men who inhabit the world of Buñuel's films, the most extreme example possibly being the obsessive husband of *El* (*He*), made in 1952 in Mexico.

8. John Hopewell, *Out of the Past* ..., p. 74, makes the point that 'Their [the hunters'] myxomatosis is Francoism'.

9. The censorship had, of course, insisted that all specific references to the Civil War be eliminated. Saura, on the other hand, proved to be an expert at, 'the need to avoid mentioning facts without evading them,' evolving an allusive technique to which the censorship could not object but which made its point very clearly.

10. In a sense Enrique is like Tristana, a *tabula rasa* exposed to influences around him.

11. See John Hopewell, *Out of the Past* ..., p. 74: 'The hunters are indeed portrayed as victims; victims, like the rabbits they shoot, precisely of their own cruelty and their fatal indifference to the feelings of others.'

Raise Ravens

The Hunt is a film deeply rooted in the aftermath of the Spanish Civil War. Eight years later, in 1973, *Cousin Angélica* proved to be, as Saura later observed, 'the film which contains the greatest number of experiences and thoughts upon the War'. It was also the film which closed a cycle in which he had grappled, albeit obliquely, with the issues and the consequences of that terrible conflict.[1] *Raise Ravens*, filmed in the months that preceded Franco's death in 1975, can be regarded as one of the first films of the transition towards democracy. The death of the central character's father, a military man who fought against the Communists, is a remarkable coincidence in the light of what was about to happen to Franco himself. For the family he leaves behind it marks the end of an era. His three children, like Spain itself, stand on the threshold of an uncertain future.

Raise Ravens was also an important moment in Saura's career in the sense that it marked the end of an association with the scriptwriter, Rafael Azcona, which went back to 1967.[2] Azcona had taught Saura much about writing scripts but by this time the director felt sufficiently confident to undertake the task alone. More than that, however, Saura was increasingly worried by Azcona's misogyny and concluded that there could be no part for a man who held such an attitude towards women in a film that would largely be about three generations of women. Although he would work again with other scriptwriters, *Raise Ravens* points to Saura's desire to be in total control of his work.

As far as the film's early history is concerned, the military raised strong objections to its presentation of an army officer as an adulterer. Their chief spokesman was the Vice-President of the Government itself, General Santiago Díaz de Mendívil. Nevertheless, in the political circumstances of the time, with Adolfo Suárez about to become President and initiate a crucial step away from military dictatorship, the protests were resisted and the Dirección General de Cinematografía backed the film. It based its argument on the grounds that Saura was by now a director of international standing and that withdrawal of the film would produce strong reaction both inside and outside Spain. Furthermore, such action would cast serious doubts on all the Government's recent statements about freedom of expression and the principles of democracy.[3]

In the event, *Raise Ravens* was shown at the Cannes Film Festival in 1976 and was awarded the Jury's Special Prize. Subsequently it proved to be a great critical and commercial success not only in Europe but also in the notoriously difficult American market. The contributions to the film's success made by the child actress, Ana Torrent, in the central role of Ana, cannot be overemphasized. Two years earlier she had appeared as another Ana in Victor Erice's outstanding film, *Spirit of the Beehive*, at the age of six. Her performance in *Raise Ravens* is one of the most brilliant in the history of the Spanish cinema and remains with the viewer long after the film has ended.

Raise Ravens begins with photographs in an album mixed in with the titles and accompanied by piano music. The photographs portray initially mother and child, followed by photographs of other children, of

mother, father and child, of father in military uniform
on a white horse, and of the three children growing up
and playing games together. The sequence ends with
individual photographs of the three girls in close-up,
looking directly at the camera, their eyes open and
receptive, their ages ranging from about five to twelve.
What precisely is its function here and how do we, the
audience, relate to it?

Our familiarity with our own family photographs
establishes an immediate link with these people we are
suddenly made to look at, and creates an interest in
them. Who is this family we have never met? What is its
history, the relationship of husband and wife, of parents and children? What kind of childhood have these
sisters had whose names we do not even know? What
are they thinking as, in the final close-ups of the sequence, they look out at us with their wide eyes? Saura
has himself made some interesting observations on
family photographs which are highly relevant here:

> In large groups there is always someone with a sad
> expression: that little girl with black hair and large
> eyes cannot conceal a complex future. On the other
> hand, there are others born with the sign of opti-
> mism written on their face and a rosy future can
> easily be predicted for them. But those who preoc-
> cupy me most are the faces which change
> substantially in the course of the family album: the
> face that was happy yesterday has in the recent
> past become sad and sensitive; that person has
> become strange and tormented in the present. In
> the future, who knows what disaster is suggested
> in the expression?[4]

The musical accompaniment has a melancholy which

may possibly relate to the family in the photographs. And what of the film's title: *Raise Ravens*? The words are part of a Spanish proverb which goes: 'Raise ravens and they'll peck out your eyes'.[5] Once more there are implications about childhood and the way in which children are shaped and influenced in the course of it. What might be called the prologue to the film is thus, for all its simplicity, wonderfully evocative and mysterious.

The first sequence proper begins to answer some of our questions but only in part. After moving across the darkened sitting room of a large bourgeois house, the camera reveals the little girl we saw in the photographs coming downstairs in her nightdress. Just before she appears, we hear a woman's voice speaking the words: 'I love you, Anselmo. You are tickling me', and then, when the child reaches the foot of the stairs, the sequence of events is precisely that which is heard and seen by her. A man's voice is heard gasping: 'I can't breathe. I'm choking'. The woman's voice calls out 'Anselmo. Anselmo!' After a few moments silence, the door of the room from which the sounds have come bursts open and a woman rushes out, attempting to button her jacket. In her haste she drops various items from her handbag, picks them up, sees the child watching her and hurries from the house. The child then enters the room where the body of a man lies on the bed, partly covered by rumpled sheets. A close-up reveals his still, staring eyes. Kneeling on the bed, the girl speaks for the first time — 'Papa', then takes a glass from the dressing-table and washes it in the kitchen.

By the end of the sequence we know some answers: the man's name is Anselmo and he is the girl's father, already seen in the family photograph. But what of the mother, and who is the woman with Anselmo? As adults we might be able to guess the answers, or some of them, but Saura's purpose here is to make us see things from the child's perspective and thus to share her sense of puzzlement. In actual fact, as we discover later, she knows the woman's identity from a previous occasion, but more important than that is her exposure here to events which are not merely traumatic but of which she has no understanding. In witnessing them as she does, we can at least feel something of the bewilderment of the child suddenly confronted with strange and terrible happenings. If, in relation to the initial photographs, we wondered about the child's formative experiences, their nature is here revealed to us in no uncertain fashion.

The two sequences that follow (though the first is really a continuation of what has been described above) have the effect, firstly, of adding to what we know already, and secondly, of taking us deeper into the child's mind. As she opens the fridge door, a woman comes into view, teasingly scolds her for being up so late, and sends her back to bed. In terms of exposition it is clear, although not stated, that the woman is the child's mother and that there is great affection between them. Moreover, although the episode is an unbroken continuation of the earlier events, the mother's appearance at a moment when her husband lies dead in the bedroom after making love with another woman suggests that this is not reality but the child's evocation of her mother, whom she greatly loves, at a moment when she needs her to cling to.

In the second of the two sequences the mother appears again and begins to comb the child's hair, taking over the task from an older woman. That this is once more an imagined episode is confirmed just afterwards when the mother leaves and the older woman, Rosa, continuing to comb the child's hair, wakes her from her daydream: 'Ana . . . Ana . . . What are you thinking about?' In addition, Ana's reply (we now know her name for the first time) is confirmation that the woman in the vision is her mother, while the past tense indicates that she is no longer here: 'Is it true that Mama always wore this cross?' That she is, in fact, dead is indicated a few moments later when, in a brief conversation on the stairs with her elder sister, Irene, Ana informs her that when she saw that her father was dead, her mother appeared in the kitchen, to which Irene replies: 'Mama is dead, Ana!' The death of the mother clearly preceded that of the father, but these are facts which, especially in the early part of the film, we, as audience, are able to put together only slowly, piece by piece. The film's structure suggests in one way the fluid, shifting nature of Ana's thoughts, in which past and present, reality and imagination are inextricably interwoven, and in another presents to its audience an intriguing mystery whose truths are only slowly revealed.

The sequence described above takes place on the day of the father's funeral. Downstairs, where the coffin lies, are military men in uniform, come to pay their last respects, as well as relatives and friends soberly dressed. It is an occasion for formality and ritual, and just before this Ana and her sisters have been prepared for it, firstly by Rosa, the family servant, who helps them to wash and dress, and secondly by another woman, their Aunt Paulina, who issues strict instructions: 'Irene, come here. When you enter the room, you first kiss your father . . . then you pray that his soul may be in heaven. . .' Paulina herself, we observe, is very formally dressed in a dark suit, her hair tightly drawn: the very image of the correctness of behaviour demanded by the occasion. The stiffness of the mourners, not unlike that of the corpse itself, cannot but bring to mind the earlier images of the woman running from the dead man's bedroom, her jacket open, and the man himself lying amongst the rumpled sheets. The contrast between the two is the contrast between private and public behaviour, which, in turn, points to the hypocrisy which denies or sweeps the former under the carpet in favour of the latter, as well as instructing the young in certain ways of conduct which have little to do with the inner person. It is not without significance that only Ana refuses to kiss her father in defiance of Aunt Paulina's instruction. Because she loved her mother and, as we see later, believes her father to be responsible for her death, Ana acts instinctively, refusing to show affection or respect for the dead man.

Shortly after the beginning of a new sequence in which Ana is seen in the garden of the house, those events which we have so far assumed to be taking place in the present are suddenly revealed as having occurred twenty years ago. A new voice is heard, the voice of an older woman, and the camera moves from a close-up of the face of Ana the child to the face of Ana at the age of about twenty-eight and remarkably similar in appearance to her dead mother (both roles were played by Geraldine Chaplin). Most of what we have seen so far consists of memories and recollections by the older Ana, and what we considered to be the memories of Ana the child are therefore the memories of the older woman of her memories as a child, the equivalent of a play within a play. Addressing the camera directly, the adult Ana wonders about the traumatic events of her childhood, and not least about her attitude towards her father. She recalls in particular how she blamed him for her mother's death and how, therefore, she had attempted to poison him with some white powder, believing, indeed, that this was what had killed him. Twenty years on, the memory of her father's guilt remains: 'The only thing I remember perfectly is that my father then seemed to be to blame for the sadness that had oppressed my mother in her last years. I was convinced that he and he alone had caused her illness and her death.' Other things, however, seem far less clear-cut than they had seemed then, the answers to the questions she continues to ask herself are 'too easy and [they] don't satisfy me'. One effect of this sudden transition in time is to underline further that feeling of uncertainty we have already experienced in the earlier part of the film by evoking the shifting, uncertain and multi-layered nature of memory itself.

If the adult Ana feels less sure about earlier certainties, her thoughts point, nevertheless, to her father's harshness and her mother's lack of freedom, both of which are to do with their respective roles in the society in which they live.[6] Indeed, it is this train of thought on Ana's part, and in particular her pondering on her mother's 'liberation' had she become a pianist,[7] which leads directly to the following sequences. In the first of these Aunt Paulina is seen correcting the children's habits at the dinner table: 'Don't you know how to behave at the table?' Paulina has now assumed the role of head of the family, taking their father's place, and is resolved to impose the same kind of discipline. A second sequence takes place in the kitchen where Ana is seen with the family servant Rosa and is less to do with the father's role as paterfamilias than with his role as a man. Rosa's opening remark, delivered in her customary matter-of-fact style, sees all men as conforming to a stereotyped pattern, as taking on the role of predators, with women as their prey: 'All men are

the same. You'll find that out when you're a woman.
They all want the same thing. Don't let them fool you.
Your father, for one: he was a real skirt-chaser.' Rosa's
role is of crucial importance; as with other servants in
so many Spanish literary or cinematic works, she sweeps
aside the niceties of bourgeois formality (consider the
old servant La Poncia in Lorca's *The House of Bernarda
Alba*), as well as shaping and helping to confirm what
Ana may so far only half believe. Of key importance in
this sequence is the window which Rosa cleans as she
talks to Ana, together with the shot in close-up of Ana,
wide-eyed, looking through it, and listening simultaneously to the sounds of the city beyond the house.[8]
The image of window and eyes come together very
suggestively to evoke the notion of the child's perception of the world. It is therefore highly significant that
at this very moment, as if conjured up by Rosa's words,
she should have a vision of her father stroking Rosa's
breasts from the other side of the glass and of herself
and her mother surprising him in the act. Earlier in the
film Ana did, of course, see another woman rush from
his bedroom, her jacket undone, and witnessed other
experiences too, as we shall see later. As a child, therefore, her ideas of what it is to be a man and what it is to
be a woman are already becoming clearly defined: her
mother's potential career and freedom abandoned in
the interests of the family; her father free to indulge his
sexual desires at his wife's expense and behind her
back.

The theme of woman as victim, brought up and
educated to accept a subordinate and often painful role,
is developed in various ways in the following sequences.
Initially, Ana listens to a pop song whose words —
'Why are you going? I wake up every night, thinking of
you. . . Why are you going?' — reflect the sadness of

her own life after her mother's death. Just afterwards she sits for a while with her grandmother who is confined to a wheelchair, unable to speak and whose only escape from her pointless life is into the past, represented by a display of photographs and an old gramophone record. In an earlier sequence Ana pushes her grandmother's wheelchair in the garden; later she sits with her again. Between the child and the old woman there is a clear link; a similarity and a difference. The grandmother, crippled and speechless, powerless to control her life,[9] looks back on experiences of which we have no knowledge but which, as a later episode suggests, may not have been particularly happy. Ana, in contrast, looks forward, not knowing what the future holds but already marked by traumatic events and conditioned to the roles of men and women. As John Hopewell has observed: 'A Francoist upbringing traumatizes; it also represses. Ana's predicament in *Cría Cuervos* is very similar to Leopoldo's in *El desencanto*: the struggle to be oneself in a society which grooms its members in social roles rather than developing their individuality.'[10]

The extent of such grooming is revealed when, with Aunt Paulina out of the house, the children play a game in which they dress as adults and in which Irene and Ana assume the roles of husband and wife. When the husband arrives home late he is questioned by the wife about his lateness, both questions and answers taking the form of familiar clichés: 'You're very late. What have you been doing until eleven o'clock?'. . . 'Please don't start. I'm worn out. I've had a heavy day.' Played by children the 'adult' confrontation is inevitably comic, but the husband's remark, 'Please, Amelia, the children', suggests how the children have in the past overheard such scenes, lying awake as the bitter accusations fly. In fact, later in the film Ana recalls such a confrontation between her own parents. The point is clearly made that the children in this and other families will become adults with preconceived ideas about adult relationships and the roles of men and women. They are indeed traumatized by their past.

For Ana as a child, the most terrible experience of all was the death of her mother; something which, her father being away, she was obliged to witness alone. Here, as in other sequences, Ana watches silently, her face almost blank and expressionless, white as a sheet of paper. We are reminded of the young Tristana about to be exposed to the bitter experiences of growing up. Ana's experience is that of seeing her mother roll in agony from one side of the bed to the other, of seeing the bloodstained sheets, of listening to her terrible moaning and desperate words, 'I'm afraid. I don't want to die.' There are some powerful images here: of Ana on the stairs and in her bedroom, hands over her ears to cut out the sound of her mother's cries; of Ana sitting on a sofa, her arms limp at her sides, eyes looking straight ahead, the record on the gramophone evoking emptiness and desolation. Ana's suffering as a child is different from her mother's but in its way equally painful. Her anguished silence as she observes her mother's death links her once more to her grandmother, mute and paralyzed. It is no surprise that the older Ana should admit, 'There are things you can't forget. It seems incredible that there are such powerful memories.'

The degree to which the memory of her mother remains with her is vividly evoked when, as she lies in bed, Ana 'sees' her standing outside the open door of her bedroom. Ana's mother then enters the room to see if she has gone to sleep and, finding she has not, tells

Ana the story of Thumbelina.[11] Ana quickly falls asleep
but wakes up again a few moments later and, finding
her mother gone, calls out to her as if she were still
alive. Her cries are answered by Aunt Paulina who
attempts to comfort her, in particular by offering to tell
her the story of Thumbelina. Ana's response is immediate and direct: 'I want you to die. I want you to die.'
However much Paulina tries to help, she cannot replace her sister. The scenes between Ana and her mother
show that there is a deep love and tenderness which
Paulina can never replace.[12] Furthermore, by taking
over the father's role as head of the family, Paulina
therefore becomes the object of Ana's resentment. Her
rejection of Paulina here is part of a more general
defiance and rebellion in the film's concluding scenes.

The first protest on Ana's part is against a developing relationship between Paulina and Nicolás, an old
officer friend of Ana's father. When Nicolás comes to
tea one day, Ana enters the room and discovers them
kissing while Nicolás confesses his deep love for Paulina.
The scene upon which Ana stumbles unintentionally is
an echo of two earlier moments in the film: of seeing
her father embracing Amelia, Nicolás's wife, during a
visit to their house in the country; and of seeing Amelia
rush from her father's bedroom at the beginning of the
film. In short, Ana views the relationship of Paulina
and Nicolás, who is still married to Amelia, as a recrea-
tion of earlier events which have brought only
unhappiness. When she points the gun at them —
which she has brought to the room for Paulina to
confirm that it was a present from her father — her
motives may well be unclear and unformulated, but
there can be no doubt that somewhere in her mind
there is a deep-seated wish to protest against a repetition in her life of what has happened once already.

The second protest is against Paulina's authoritari-
anism. In a scene in the kitchen where Paulina is using
the sewing-machine, Rosa begins to talk to Ana about
her mother, telling the child how much like her she is
becoming, how undeservedly her mother suffered, what
a saint she was. Rosa's words, uttered in Paulina's
presence, are undoubtedly a deliberate provocation,
motivated in part by Rosa's affection for her former
mistress whom she attended faithfully during her suffering, and by resentment towards her new mistress.[13]
At all events, Paulina orders Rosa from the room and
then, seeing her authority challenged and possibly
undermined, loses her temper with Ana. It is this that
finally leads Ana to try to poison her with the same
harmless powder she believes killed her father.

The ending of the film marks both the end of the
school holidays and a new stage in Ana's life.[14] When
morning comes, she is amazed to discover that Paulina
is not dead. Her attempt to destroy her authority and
her influence upon her life has failed. Moreover, it is
now time to return to school, where Paulina's bourgeois values of discipline, obedience and submission,
of what it is to be a woman in a society which changes
little in its attitudes, will further chip away at Ana's
independent spirit.

Raise Ravens is undoubtedly a remarkable film. Much
more complex structurally than *The Hunt*, its flash-
backs and unexpected leaps in time make it a fascinating,
teasing and arresting film to watch. In suggesting the
way in which a child is shaped by the events to which
it is exposed, Saura's achievement is of the highest
order.

Notes

1. In an interview with José Oliver, *Cambio 16*, no. 284, May 1977, p. 101.

2. See, in particular, Agustín Sánchez Vidal, *El cine de Carlos Saura* . . ., pp. 98–99.

3. See Agustín Sánchez Vidal, p. 98.

4. Saura's observations on the subject of the family album can be found in *L'Avant-Scène du Cinéma*, no. 214, October 1978, p. 5, and in an interview in *Cuadernos para el diálogo*, no. 211, May 1977, p. 79. The translation into English is my own.

5. John Hopewell, *Out of the Past* . . ., p. 139, suggests that 'The most obvious reference in the title is to Ana's rebellion against her upbringing (Paulina calls the sisters "crías" — literally "young creatures").' Virginia Higginbotham, *Spanish Film under Franco* . . ., p. 92, notes that 'Saura's choice of a proverb for the title of this film is an accurate reflection of fascist use of language. . . The rancorous prediction of this particular proverb is especially typical of a repressive, fearful and conformist myth such as that of the Franco regime.' Central to that regime, of course, was the concept of the family and of bringing up one's children to believe in the 'correct' values.

6. Virginia Higginbotham, *op. cit.*, p. 94, suggests that 'as the child becomes the mother, her hopes, too, will fade since women's lives in Spain have not changed for generations.'

7. There is a certain autobiographical element here inasmuch as Saura's mother had chosen to bring up a family rather than pursue a career as a professional pianist.

8. John Hopewell, *Out of the Past* . . ., p. 139, makes the point that 'the children's domestic education denies them their eyes as a faculty for communication.'

9. Virginia Higginbotham, *Spanish Film under Franco* . . ., p. 94, argues that 'Her role is a mute testament to the fact that women in a paternalistic society are not only confined as the grandmother is to her wheelchair . . . to the home as the only domain — but are without voice in the Franco dictatorship.'

10. John Hopewell, *Out of the Past* . . ., p. 138.

11. Another autobiographical touch, for Saura has stated that the Thumberlina story was the only bed-time story his mother ever knew.

12. In relation to the sequence where Paulina has lunch with the children, Peter Evans has drawn attention to her coldness. See '*Cría cuervos* and the Daughters of Fascism', *Vida Hispánica*, 33, 1984, pp. 17–22. Despite some attempts to be pleasant to the children, her coldness and formality characterizes her throughout the film.

13. There are several occasions on which Paulina refers to the chaotic state of the house prior to her arrival.

14. See Agustín Sánchez Vidal, *El cine de Carlos Saura* . . ., p. 103.

Carmen

Carmen was completed in 1983, the second of three 'musicals' of great distinction, the first being *Blood Wedding (Bodas de sangre)* in 1981 and the third *Love the Magician (El amor brujo)* in 1986. The idea for the film had occurred some years earlier when Saura had been given a copy of Prosper Mérimée's original story, but took more concrete form when, after making *Blood Wedding*, the producer, Emiliano Piedra, suggested to Saura that they make another film on the same lines. Saura had been attracted to making a film of Lorca's famous play after seeing it in a flamenco version performed by the company of Antonio Gades, whose work he admired for its discipline, its precision, its physical grace and its expression of 'popular tradition in its truest sense.' He had no hesitation, therefore, in seizing the opportunity to work with Gades once more. Prior to this he had, in fact, rejected an approach from Gaumont to film Bizet's opera (the film was subsequently made by Francesco Rosi) precisely because he had his own ideas for the treatment of the Carmen story. These consisted of taking Mérimée, not Bizet, as his point of departure, and of placing the story firmly in the context of flamenco dance. In addition, Saura was attracted by the idea of updating the story by interweaving the traditional tale with that of a present-day Carmen, which would have a particular resonance not only in an age of feminist attitudes but in a Spain in which the traditional role of woman was rapidly changing. At all events, in both commercial and critical terms *Carmen* proved to be a great success, running in New York for eight successive months. Nominated for an Oscar in 1984, it lost out to Bergman's *Fanny and Alexander* but at the Cannes Film Festival it was awarded the prize for artistic merit. *Carmen* received much praise too in Europe, not least in Germany, and in Tokyo was seen by 73,000 people in the space of two weeks.[1]

As far as the two principal sources of the film are concerned, Saura greatly admired Mérimée's story of 1845, not merely for its skillful creation of a Spanish setting and atmosphere but also for its totally convincing protagonist. Bizet's opera, on the other hand, despite its wonderful music, both refined the character of Carmen herself and contained a somewhat prettified and false picture of Spain:

> The opera *Carmen* is in a sense a betrayal of Mérimée's story. . . The 'local colour' derives from Bizet, not from Mérimée, and perhaps mainly from the librettists, Meihac and Helévy. . . They realized how risky it was to put on the stage a woman who is a thief, witch, whore, and almost a murderess. . . a woman, moreover, who mocks conventional morality and adopts an attitude to life which borders on anarchism. . . I believe that the opera has eliminated the violence and sensuality, the mystery, and even the justification for a form of behaviour which in Mérimée is perfectly comprehensible and does not need to be justified. Carmen is what she is. Carmen is not a conventional woman, for she symbolizes freedom, although that freedom may demand that she sacrifice others, steal or prostitute herself. . .[2]

Saura's purpose, therefore, was in part to restore to Carmen those characteristics which the opera had underplayed and, in addition, to locate the story in an authentic Spanish setting.

Carmen begins with a sequence which precedes the titles and in which a group of female dancers are put through a series of flamenco steps by Antonio, the director of a dance company. The camera then moves from the dancers themselves to Antonio, who is observing them, and they are now seen in the great mirror which occupies one of the end walls of the rehearsal room. Finally, we see the dancers once more through Antonio's eyes, the camera moving from one girl to another as they individually perform certain flamenco movements. At the end of the sequence Antonio expresses his sense of disappointment that none of the dancers seem suitable for the role of Carmen and observes that the search will have to continue in Seville.

This 'prologue' to the film sets out very clearly Saura's principal aims and objectives in *Carmen*. Firstly, it asserts the importance of flamenco dance and, in conjunction with it, its intention to place the story of Carmen in an authentic Spanish context and setting. Secondly, the point is made that Antonio, searching for the ideal dancer to play the part of Carmen, has in his head an image, a stereotyped concept of what she is: an idea which is central to the film as a whole and which is reinforced here by the image of the dancers in the mirror. And thirdly, since the dancers are real women, dressed casually in modern clothes, there is already a pointer to the fact that one of Saura's aims will be to contemporize the Carmen story, bridging the gap between past and present, fiction and reality. Indeed, the fact that Antonio has in his head an image of Carmen anticipates the way in which he — as a man and by extension other Spanish men — has a preconceived idea of what he wants a woman to be in reality, be it as a lover, a wife or a whore.

The titles themselves are projected against a series of engravings from the past and accompanied by Bizet's music.[3] In contrast to the prologue's emphasis on Spanish authenticity, both engravings and music represent foreigners' views and interpretations of Spain: in the engravings; for example, the dancers have tambourines, which play no part in genuine flamenco. When the titles end and are immediately replaced by another sequence in the dance studio in which the women are joined by male dancers, the 'foreign' section is seen to be framed on either side by a tradition which could not be more Spanish. In addition to the stamping of feet, further percussive sounds are now introduced by the beating of sticks on the floor, which in turn becomes flamenco singing and flamenco guitar. A key moment occurs when Antonio puts on the stereo a tape recording of the *seguidilla* from Act I of Bizet's opera and the famous flamenco guitarist, Paco de Lucía, begins to adapt it to the requirements of the guitar.[4] In short, as the music of the opera is changed and adapted to an authentic Spanish musical instrument and a genuine Spanish musical tradition, the orchestra and voice are replaced by guitar and clapping. This adapted music accompanies the dance performed by Antonio and Cristina, dance teachers of the company. A series of movements performed by the female dancers follows, characterized by the beautiful, graceful patterns created by hands and arm: a key part of flamenco dance. At the end of the sequence Mérimée's words are introduced in the form of Antonio's thoughts: 'Carmen had a wild and strange beauty . . . her lips full and well-shaped. . . Gypsy eyes, wolf eyes. . .' Snatches of

Mérimée's text and echoes of Bizet's music are therefore present but placed within the framework of flamenco
dance. The story of Carmen is thus returned to Spain.[5]

This process occupies much of the early part of the
film and is extended by two further sequences. The first
of these is set in a dance school in Seville where a
flamenco teacher, Magdalena, is instructing her pupils.
The essential characteristics of flamenco dance are captured in her instructions: 'Heads up. . . [Arms] up . . .
slowly . . . like an eagle's wings. . . ' And again: 'The
breasts like a bull's horns but warm and soft. . . The
head up, the posture princely.' In the second, Cristina
(the famous Spanish flamenco dancer, Cristina Hoyos)
is teaching flamenco to Carmen, the dancer chosen by
Antonio to play the part of Carmen. As in the earlier
sequence, emphasis is placed on posture and hand-
movements: 'Your hands . . . fluttering like doves. . .
The body upright . . . like a queen.' The effect of the
first twenty minutes or so of the film is therefore to
establish the essentially Spanish background, in all its
purity, within which the story of Carmen will unfold.
In contrast to this, we are shown at one point the night-
club in which Carmen the dancer normally works,
performing flamenco for foreign tourists. In the context
of the pure, disciplined form of dance elaborated upon
in so much detail, this is extremely sloppy; a kind of
packaged flamenco for foreigners, and thus, like aspects of Bizet's opera, to be rejected.

As far as the fictional Carmen is concerned, Saura's
intention was to reject the prettified and toned-down
version of the opera in favour of Mérimée's much more
earthy original.[6] Mérimée's experience of Spain was
considerable and his love of its people and customs
deep and passionate. In his story of Carmen he not only
recreated the surface detail of Spanish low life but

presented to the reader a woman who is as convincing to the reader as she obviously was to Don José and all her other admirers; untrustwothy, unpredictable and ultimately fascinating in all her contradictions. He placed her, moreover, in settings which cannot in any way be described as glamorous, as in the case of the tobacco factory:

> When I went into the hall I was confronted with three hundred women, wearing their shifts or very little more, and all shrieking, howling, gesticulating, and making such a noise that you couldn't have heard God's thunder. To one side of them a woman was lying on her back, covered with blood, and with a cross on her face which had just been carved with two strokes of a knife. Opposite the wounded woman, who was being looked after by the rest of the group, I saw Carmen being held by five or six of her cronies. . .[7]

In contrast, Bizet both refined and glamorized the story and the character of Carmen, although it has to be said that he was also much constrained by the taste and conventions of the Paris Opéra-Comique of the late nineteenth century.[8] A particularly good example of this is the omission of the fight in the tobacco factory, which is reported rather than seen. In the opera Don José is a less violent and passionate character, Carmen his only victim, while in Mérimée's story he also kills a lieutenant and Carmen's husband, García. Mérimée's bullfighter, Lucas, had only a small part, but in the opera the role of Escamillo was greatly expanded, no doubt because the bullfight was considered by Bizet's librettists to be typically Spanish and especially glamorous. Finally, of course, there is the character of Carmen herself. Prior to this the heroines of nineteenth-century opera had invariably embodied chaste and pure love, in the light of which Bizet's creation was both new and shocking. Nevertheless, she remains a toned-down version of Mérimée's original.

In the film Saura's predilection for Mérimée is often revealed by the way in which quotations from his story are used to introduce particular sequences. Antonio's discovery of Carmen the dancer in Seville, for example, is accompanied by the words of Mérimée's text: 'I looked up and saw her. . . . It was a Friday. . . . I'll never forget it. . . . But she, following the habit of women and cats who do not call. . . .'

In contrast, the clichéd version of Spain presented by the opera is mocked and rejected, as one sequence in particular reveals. On the occasion of Antonio's birthday, his dancers present him with a parodied version of moments from the opera. When Carmen enters, the comb, the huge earrings and the large fan are all exaggerated forms of the foreigner's idea of Spain. When Cristina 'challenges' Carmen by exposing her buttocks, it is a mock version of the confrontation in the tobacco factory. All this is then capped by the entry of the bullfighter to the strains of Bizet's music. The individual playing the bullfighter wears a comic hat, is greeted by comic whistles, uses a member of the company as a horse and a walking stick as a sword. His subsequent triumphal march sees him being carried aloft outside and Antonio kissing him through the glass of the great window in a final parodic gesture.

While the restoration of the Carmen story to a genuine Spanish background and of the character herself to a more primitive and credible form are two of the film's outstanding features, its final triumph lies in the relationship of the story to contemporary reality and, in formal and structural terms, in the increasing overlapping of fiction and reality as the action unfolds. From the moment when Antonio encounters the dancer, Carmen, in the dance school in Madrid, the process is set in motion, for a real woman called Carmen is to play the fictional Carmen, and she, moreover, is chosen by Antonio because she possesses in reality those characteristics which Antonio associates with her fictional counterpart. Shortly after this, moreover, there is a sequence in which Cristina instructs Carmen the dancer in the art of flamenco in front of a mirror which reflects her image.[9] The idea of two Carmens, the one a replica of the other, is thus reinforced visually, while in a later sequence we see both Carmen and Antonio similarly reflected as two pairs of lovers: the real Carmen and Antonio and the fictional lovers, Carmen and Don José, whom they are at this precise moment playing.

The interplay and overlap is implied in the early stages of the film and later made indistinguishable. In an early sequence, for example, Antonio is dissatisfied with his pupil's progress and urges her to become more focussed and aggressive: 'Devour me!' His words, which are to do with her playing of the role, have implications for their real-life relationship which at this moment he does not understand. A little later Antonio describes to the dancers what occurred after the fight in the tobacco factory and, in particular, Carmen's promises to Don José. He refers to Mérimée's text: 'She lied. Sir, she has always lied. . . . I don't know if she ever spoke a word of truth. But when she spoke I believed her. I could not help it'. As he speaks the words, he looks at Carmen the dancer, transforming fiction into a potential but as yet unproven reality.[10]

The process is further advanced when Carmen the dancer visits Antonio at night in the dance studio. Just as in a dance sequence immediately preceding this the fictional Carmen takes the initiative in relation to Don José, so does the real Carmen by going to see Antonio. Her arrival is accompanied by the love theme from Bizet's opera heard in the preceding fictional scene. For the first time in the film fiction and reality are specifically interwoven. When, moreover, Carmen joins Antonio on the stage and begins to dance with him, her words 'Devour me!' are quickly transformed from something to do with artistic performance into an act of passion as he embraces and kisses her. Later that night Antonio wakes up to find Carmen about to leave and fails to persuade her to tell him why. It is a moment in which the real-life Carmen becomes her fictional counterpart by asserting her independence.

The two levels are fused most completely and brilliantly in the scenes concerning Antonio and Carmen the dancer's husband after his release from prison.[11] In the studio a group of dancers, which also includes Carmen's husband, are involved in a game of cards which ends abruptly when Antonio accuses him of cheating. They confront each other and then, it would seem, resolve their differences in a violent fight with sticks, at the end of which the husband is overcome and Carmen removes her wedding ring, throwing it to the floor beside him. Only after this, when the husband rises and removes his wig, do we suddenly realize that the whole of the fight with sticks is fictional, not real, and that the husband here is not the person involved in the game of cards but a dancer disguised to look remarkably like him. It is a brilliant moment which points to the fact that, for Antonio and Carmen, fiction and reality are now indistinguishable.[12] At the film's climax they totally coincide.

When Carmen attempts to break away from Antonio,

she is dressed in modern clothes and walks past stacked chairs and dancers who are sitting and smoking — all reminders of reality but also of performance and therefore fiction. At the same time, as Antonio (or is it Don José?) pursues and stabs her, the sound-track consists of the 'Fate' theme from Bizet's opera. As he stands over her dead body, Antonio is Don José and Don José Antonio, fiction made truth in the most painful and illuminating manner.

The fusion of fiction and truth, of a story from the past with a story from the present, is not simply a clever artistic tour de force, for it also allows Saura to explore the sexual status of women in post-Franco Spain. As we have seen already, both *The Hunt* and *Raise Ravens* present women as victims, imprisoned in traditional roles and manipulated by male attitudes. In contrast, *Carmen* is about a woman who is free, the fictional character acting as a kind of role model for her modern counterpart. In the sequence in which Antonio discovers her with another man in the costume department, Carmen the dancer states her position very clearly: 'Let go of me!. . . . I'm free! I'll do what I want!. . . . I didn't promise you anything! You have no right to ask me!' Antonio, however, is still rooted in the past, a prisoner of traditional male attitudes which see women as sex objects, as possessions which are theirs and no one else's. In short, the Carmen-Antonio relationship embodies the dilemma confronting the modern Spanish woman as she strives for her independence.[13] In Buñuel's *Tristana* the protagonist obtains her freedom at considerable cost. In *Carmen* she pays for it by being murdered.

As well as reinterpreting the story, Saura also concentrates on episodes which focus on the conflicting passions of love, jealousy and rivalry. The sequence in the tobacco factory is a particularly striking example.

Bizet, it will be recalled, omitted the scene, preferring to report rather than portray it, while Mérimée's account was distinguished by its realism. When Antonio prepares his dancers to rehearse the scene, he therefore evokes, without directly quoting Mérimée, the realistic feel and atmosphere of the place: '. . . we are in Seville in 1830, in the tobacco factory. . . . It's very hot. Only women work there, they make themselves comfortable. . . .' Clearly, there is nothing pretty or glamorous here. The sequence begins with hands beating rhythmically on tables, setting up the rhythmic pulse of the scene, while the women who create the rhythm are genuine gypsies and in no way glamorized. When they begin to sing over the rhythmic beat, the camera tracks across their faces in close-up, emphasizing their rawness, as if we were observing a painting by Goya. The song initiated by these women is then taken up by the whole group, assuming an even greater momentum. Cristina, playing one of the factory girls, rises from the table, moves to the centre of the room and issues a challenge to Carmen in the form of a vigorous dance. Accepting the challenge, Carmen confronts Cristina. The excitement generated by the accelerating rhythm of hands and feet is underpinned by brilliant camerawork, close-ups of faces and expressions, cutting quickly to the group as a whole and overhead shots. This matches the swirling, kaleidoscopic effect of the dance itself as all the women join in and fall into two opposing groups. Finally, Carmen produces a knife, slashes Cristina across the throat, and the dancing stops suddenly and dramatically.

If Bizet omitted the scene, Saura, taking Mérimée as his source, gives it pride of place. And because there is no operatic music to take into account, Saura employs his own: the pure, stark music of flamenco created entirely by hands, feet and voice. If, in the early part of the film, the purpose is to set out the essential characteristics of flamenco dance and song, and in so doing to create a genuinely Spanish background, this crucial scene is now set firmly in that background, the story returned to authentic Seville, heartland of flamenco itself. Secondly, in this episode the character of Carmen is very much restored to Mérimée's original. In the dance section she is beautiful, proud, dangerous, aggressive and ultimately ruthless. Afterwards, arrested by Don José, she is alluring, tempting and manipulative: in short, a much more rounded and complex young woman than is suggested by Bizet's opera. And thirdly, although the sequence in the tobacco factory is the first of the four episodes presented in detail by Saura, it already suggests that overlap of fiction and reality that becomes so important later on. In the 'modern' story, for example, jealousy leads to the confrontation with Cristina who, informed by Antonio that he needs someone younger to play the part of Carmen, is jealous of the dancer Carmen both on that account and because Antonio is increasingly attracted to her as a woman. Again, after her arrest by Don José, Carmen begins to entice and tempt him. In reality, as Carmen and Antonio rehearse this particular moment, the camera isolates them from the rest of the dancers, not only focussing on their facial expressions but also blurring the distinction between the parts they play and the feelings they experience as people. Isolated from the others, they live only for each other.

The final bullfight sequence is also worthy of detailed consideration. From the outset it is never clear to what extent this is a rehearsal, to what extent reality. The presence of the bullfighter, initially seen trying on his costume and practising with his cloak, alone seems to tell us that this is theatre. Otherwise, everyone wears their everyday clothes, so that when Carmen dances with the bullfighter and Antonio observes them suspiciously, it is impossible to know whether he does so as Antonio or as Don José. Moreover, the famous and instantly recognizable 'toreador' music of Bizet, which would suggest that this is theatre, is rejected in favour of a *pasodoble*, which not only establishes a Spanish authenticity but projects the impression that the dance is a real one. As well as the *pasodoble*, flamenco also plays a notable part, particularly in the song about love:

> 'Love is awful and jealousy treacherous. . .
> If I'm dying, jealousy is to blame. . .
> Poor lover, eaten by jealousy. . .
> From dawn to sunset, jealousy will devour him. . .
> Jealousy is to blame for cowardly acts. . .
> Jealousy is a burning, devouring fire. . .
> Love and jealousy belong to the same kin. . .
> Poor lover . . . no one to pity you!'[14]

If the words apply to Don José, they apply with equal force to Antonio as he moves restlessly through the crowd, unable to control his feelings. In the early part of the film the mirror allowed us to see a double image, in effect the dancer and the part being played. In the later part of the film, as far as Carmen and Antonio are concerned, there is no mirror, no double image, for the two are by now one, the person and the part identical.

The second film in Saura's musical trilogy, *Carmen*, is indisputably the best of the three films. The earlier *Blood Wedding* is in its own way a great achievement, a fine transposition to flamenco dance of a famous and powerful work for the stage. But what gives *Carmen* its extra edge and special resonance is the cunning inter-weaving of its two stories, of Carmen projected into modern times, of art transformed into life. It has been suggested that, with the end of the dictatorship in 1975, many of those artists who worked within and against it, using its excesses as material for their work, have subsequently floundered in the vacuum of democracy. Saura, as *Carmen* proves, continues to explore themes and issues from earlier films — in particular the role of women — albeit in a changing context.

N o t e s

1. For the background to the film see Agustín Sánchez Vidal, *El cine de Carlos Saura . . .*, pp. 182–85.

2. Carlos Saura, 'Historia de nuestra película', in *Carmen*, Barcelona: Círculo/Folio, 1984, pp. 55–56.

3. The engravings are by Gustave Doré.

4. For a discussion of the 'Spanish' character of Bizet's music, see Gwynne Edwards, 'Carmen', in *Catholic Tastes and Times: Essays in Honour of Michael E. Williams*, Leeds: Trinity and All Saints' College, 1987, pp. 127–155. On flamenco the reader is recommended to *El arte del baile flamenco*, Barcelona: Ediciones Polígrafa, 1977.

5. In *Challenges to Authority: Fiction and Film in Contemporary Spain*, London: Tamesis, 1988, Peter Evans and Robin Fiddian argue in their chapter on *Carmen* that Saura's film 'europeanizes' the story. My own view is clearly the opposite.

6. Antonio Gades, 'Historia de nuestra película'. . ., p. 169, observes that although he and Saura listened to the

opera on many occasions, it was the *novella* of Mérimée which they found more interesting.

7. See the edition of the story by M.J. Tilby in *Prosper Mérimée, Carmen et autres nouvelles choisies*, London: Harrap, 1981. The translation is my own.

8. On the history of the opera, see Winton Dean, *Bizet*, London: J.M. Dent, 1965, pp. 212–38.

9. The mirror is a favourite Saura device and is used in his films for a variety of purposes. In *Blood Wedding*, for example, the image reflected in it reminds the individual that he or she is seen in a certain way by other members of the community, i.e., that image is important.

10. On the interplay of fiction and reality, see too John Hopewell, *Out of the Past . . .*, pp. 155–57.

11. John Hopewell, *Out of the Past . . .*, p. 155, suggests that Antonio 'imagines Carmen going to jail to visit her husband.' I cannot see that this is the case. Since her husband is in jail, there is no reason why she should not visit him in reality.

12. The other important point about the fight sequence is that its simplicity and starkness highlight its ritualistic character, thereby giving it a universal quality, like a duel in a Western.

13. John Hopewell, *Out of the Past . . .*, p. 154, makes the valid point that 'male-female relations have not evolved substantially beyond the Spain which Mérimée found in the nineteenth century. . . .'

14. The words of the song are simple and to the point, communicating very directly the emotions that inspire them, just as the austerity of flamenco does. There is nothing superfluous or glamorous here, as is the case in the bullfight scene in Bizet's opera.

Ay, Carmela!

Made in 1990, *Ay, Carmela!* was Saura's twenty-third feature-length film and, in his own words, the first in which he was able to treat the subject of the Civil War with any kind of humour:

> I would have been incapable a few years ago of treating our Civil War with humour . . . but now it is different, for sufficient time has passed to adopt a broader perspective, and there is no doubt that by employing humour it is possible to say things that it would be more difficult if not impossible to say in another way. . . .[1]

In his earlier films allusions to the war and to its consequences are characterized by violence and brutality, and if there is any humour at all it is grim and ironic. One of the most surprising and arresting features of *Ay, Carmela!* is that, despite the fact that the action is set fully in the War, Saura's treatment of it should employ such a wide range of comic effects, including farce.

The film is based on the play of the same name by the Valencian dramatist, José Sanchís Sinisterra. Highly successful in recent years in Spain, the play focuses entirely on the two principal characters, Carmela and Paulino, and tells their story largely in flash-back.[2] When it begins, Paulino is alone and depressed, for Carmela is already dead, the victim of a fascist bullet at their last performance as variety artistes. In the first part of the play Carmela returns as a ghost to converse with Paulino, blaming him for all that has happened, and in the second part to evoke in detail the fatal performance. Containing only two characters and a single setting, the play conforms, despite its considerable ingenuity, to the demands of a theatre staged in difficult economic circumstances which could not be less suited to cinematic treatment.

In adapting the play, Saura has made precisely this point: the cinema has its own language and is able to portray things which would be impossible in the theatre.[3] His aim was, therefore, to open up the story and, in particular, to present it not in flash-back but in a linear manner.[4] In effect, this allowed Saura to follow the journey of Carmela and Paulino during the two days in which they travel from Republican to Nationalist territory, performing their act in both camps. It also allowed much more scope for the relationship and the characters of Carmela and Paulino to evolve, as it were, before our eyes and in relation to the events in which they find themselves caught up. Of course, it also enabled Saura to depict other characters and locations which are only mentioned in the play, in particular Gustavete, the travelling companion of Carmela and Paulino, and the Italian officer and theatre director, Lieutenant Amelio di Ripamonte. In terms of location, the towns where the action occurs, particular places within those towns, and the theatre in which the final third of the film is located are also depicted. In the end it has to be said that Sinisterra's play seems decidedly small-scale in comparison with the sense of space, the high emotions, the feeling of great events occurring, and the epic sweep of Saura's film.

As the titles appear, the camera pans over ruined

buildings, men sitting amongst sandbags and tattered posters flapping on walls. At the end of the sequence, a title informs us: 'The Nationalist Army, supported by Italian troops, has opened a new offensive in Aragón. . . . The Aragonese front, 1938. The Republican Army desperately holds positions. . . .' In contrast to the visual evocation of the grim destruction caused by war, the title-song, 'Ay, Carmela', which is heard on the soundtrack, has a light, jaunty, joyful quality.[5] The opening sequence thus introduces the two contrasting moods, the mixture of light and dark, which characterize the film as a whole, and in particular its shattering conclusion.

The first third of *Ay, Carmela!* sees its three principal characters, Carmela, Paulino and the mute Gustavete —dumb as the result of an explosion—in the Aragonese town of Montejo, where they are entertaining Republican troops with their variety act. Paulino proceeds to introduce Carmela to the audience: 'Carmela and Paulino, tip-top variety, performing here for the first time, and also in the vanguard of the victorious front, have great pleasure in presenting this musical extravaganza with that shining star of Spanish music hall, subject of world-wide acclaim, the inimitable and one and only, the stunning and extraordinary, Carmela!' There is something comic about Paulino's overblown introduction of Carmela which we instantly recognize as the self-indulgent and harmless propaganda of show business. Later in the film the same kind of inflated language is used by the Nationalists for purely political ends, and although still comic in its sheer ostentation, is seen to be humourless and dangerous. The power of words, and the meaning of words in a given context, are amongst the film's most important themes.

The variety act, consisting of four items, is beautifully

shot, and in its changing moods is typical of the film in general. It begins with Carmela singing a traditional song: 'I wouldn't exchange the extravagance and dash, nor the enchantment of a Sevillian night, no, I wouldn't, for the fine breeding and dash of my prancer from Jérez. Sitting in this saddle, I am a queen, diamond spurs at my heels, and on my head, for a crown, a cheery Cordoban hat. . . .' Dressed in a long red dress, Carmela performs with great gusto, accompanying the words of the song with a lively dance and involving her enthusiastic and excited audience in the performance.[6] Suddenly, however, the mood changes completely. The sound of approaching Nationalist planes brings silence where there was noise, apprehension where there was joy. And then they are gone again, and Paulino's reading of a poem by Antonio Machado introduces a note of patriotic fervour which, if it seems quaint and outmoded now, clearly represents the feelings of the Republicans in 1938. But the seriousness of this moment immediately gives way to farce when, at the request of the audience, Paulino is obliged to perform his routine 'The Farts', in which he twists himself into a variety of ridiculous postures in an attempt to break wind. The fourth and final item is, in contrast, much more serious, for Carmela now appears in a white dress, holding aloft the scales of justice, while Paulino brandishes the Republican flag and they sing a song whose theme is freedom. In this initial sequence Saura evokes quite beautifully a series of changing moods which reflect both the high emotions and the uncertainties and sudden dangers of war. The shifts of mood and emotion are, moreover, effortlessly suggested, the work of a film-maker whose touch is absolutely sure. Suffice it to say that we are at every stage drawn into the reality of this film as though it were happening here and now.

Such are the dangers and deprivations they encounter that Paulino suggests they head for Valencia, for which they require petrol. Their attempt to obtain it and the beginning of the journey itself involves both a wonderfully comic scene and an insight into the relationship of Carmela and Paulino which develops as the film unfolds. As to the first point, Carmela is required to distract a Republican lorry driver while Paulino and Gustavete siphon off the petrol. She does so by climbing into his cab, but is not really prepared for his request that she allow him to squeeze her breasts. We are thus presented with the highly comic spectacle of Paulino and Gustavete making off with the petrol while Carmela, who somewhat earlier had played on stage the symbolic and pure figure of justice, is having her breast felt by a Republican who at this moment is not exactly fired by political idealism. In addition, the episode points already to the fact that it is Carmela who takes the initiative, who is both braver, more long-suffering and less selfish than Paulino. On the second point, the difficult journey on the road to Valencia on a misty night when Paulino is almost falling asleep, involves him in frequent petty arguments with Carmela which characterize their relationship throughout the film but which at the same time reveal the genuine love and affection that exist between them. Different from each other in many ways, impatient with each other, often provoked into squabbles by the difficult nature of their circumstances, they are presented on screen with great conviction and are brilliantly played by Carmen Maura and Andrés Pajares. Their relationship, presented in great detail and with utter conviction, is one of the film's many triumphs.

The second part of the film begins with their arrest by Nationalist troops and initiates a series of episodes in which the mixture of serious and comic elements is constant, complex and brilliantly balanced. On the one hand, as in the case of their interrogation by a Nationalist officer, their situation is potentially dangerous and desperate, the presence of a Republican flag in their van incriminating, the manner of the officer cold, aloof and entirely humourless. It is hardly the stuff of comedy, yet comedy there is, inspired by the very humourlessness of the officer, an unsmiling advocate of patriotic cliché, and the discomfort and desperation of Carmela, Paulino and Gustavete, uncertain as to how they should respond to him. Carmela, for example, attempts to explain the presence of the flag: 'They lent it to us for a number. It wasn't funny and Christ knows. . . .' Cut short immediately by the officer for whom the Church is part of the cause for which he is fighting — 'Leave Christ out of it!' — Carmela desperately backtracks: 'Yes, sir, he's out of it.' At the end of the sequence Paulino, without believing at all in what he is doing, makes a great show of saluting Franco, and Gustavete hurriedly chalks on his slate, 'Long live Spain!' This is the first example of many in the film in which comedy is squeezed from the fears and uncertainties of people under pressure, desperately seeking a way out. The fact that it works depends to a large extent on the degree to which we ourselves believe in and sympathize with them in their predicaments.

The way in which comedy alternates with episodes of extraordinary grimness is illustrated perfectly when the three prisoners are taken to the school which is now, ironically, a prison camp where Republicans are being held and, as it were, 'taught' the error of their ways. Shots of driving rain, ruined buildings, prisoners huddled together, haunted, frightened, silent faces, build up a detailed picture of the harshness and the

horror of war, underlined at every stage by the unrelieved
emphasis on dark colours and the insistent and menacing drumbeat on the soundtrack.[7] Exterior shots are
replaced in turn by the schoolroom where, instead of
pupils sitting at their desks, weary and frightened men
and women are now slumped over them, the scene
enveloped in the silence of despair. Apart, that is, from
Carmela who is talking to a Polish soldier, a member of
the International Brigade. As she does so, the door
suddenly bursts open, a group of Nationalists enter,
and Republicans are picked out, in an atmosphere of
mounting tension and terror, to be taken away and
shot. Carmela herself, normally bright and cheerful, is
reduced to panic. Gustavete, his inability to speak so
effective here in that his feelings are registered entirely
in facial expressions and gestures, writes desperately
on his slate. The emotions of the characters have their
counterpart in the steady drumbeat and the sustained
chords on the soundtrack, voices outside bark com-
mands, and finally gun-fire fills the air as the prisoners
are executed. The sequence is superbly handled in
every respect, building relentlessly to its shattering
climax.

It is the darkness of this powerful sequence which
largely creates the comedy of the next one as Carmela,
Paulino and Gustavete are driven away in an army car.
Convinced that they are about to be shot, the horror of
the episode in the schoolroom fresh in their minds,
their reactions of panic and desperation are completely
understandable but become, in the context, extremely
comic. This, in part, is enhanced by the fact that the
driver is an Italian who cannot understand Paulino's
questions, in consequence of which Paulino is driven to
even greater lengths to ingratiate himself: 'Italian and
Spanish, friends ... Mussolini, great man. . . .' But at

the heart of much of the comedy is the fact that Paulino is not a hero but a small, very ordinary man who merely wants to survive. As such, he is driven by very ordinary feelings which force him to desperate measures to save his own skin. All human pretensions to bravery and dignity fly out of the window.

In addition, Gustavete's inability to speak as the result of a bomb blast is in itself touching, but his reactions to situations such as that in which the three now find themselves are expressed in purely physical terms: anguished expressions, physical movements, agitated writing on his slate, in short the language of silent film. When, therefore, Paulino and Gustavete are together in shot, their similar reaction to situations of danger are expressed in totally opposite ways, which creates a wonderfully comic juxtaposition.

A particularly brilliant and sustained comic sequence begins when the Italian driver deposits them, much to their surprise and bewilderment, at the Teatro Goya, where they are led into the presence of an Italian officer. When he questions them about their activities in Republican territory and, in particular, about their use of the flag in their show, they are convinced that they are soon to be court-martialled and are desperate to convince him that they are merely innocent performers. Their act is now performed for him but in an unspoken panic which makes it quite hilarious: Carmela, wrapped in the flag, exposes one breast, which Paulino fumbles to cover up. The officer's surprise and embarrassment draws from him a compliment on the beauty of Carmela's bosom: 'My compliments. Beautiful!' Gustavete, on all fours and pawing the air, mimes the lion at the feet of justice, and Paulino, eager to impress, suddenly bursts into 'O, Sole mio', which the officer immediately takes up. These are all exquisitely comic moments, but equally comic is the fact that the fear and panic which underlies and motivates them are themselves based on a misunderstanding. In reality, the Italian officer has summoned the three not so much for questioning as to use them to entertain the Nationalist officers and troops at a forthcoming concert. There is also the added irony that, despite their panic, or perhaps because of it, Carmela, Paulino and Gustavete have performed so well that they have succeeded in totally convincing the officer of their acting ability. And finally there is the comedy born not of desperation but of relief when they realize they are not to be shot after all. When the officer announces himself to be Lieutenant Amelio di Ripamonte, 'in civilian life a famous theatre director', Paulino's words come tumbling out, a torrent of exaggeration capped with a wonderful and unintentionally incongruous juxtaposition of names: '. . . Italy, the cradle of art. You've got Michaelangelo, Dante, Petrarch, Puccini, Rossini, Boccherini, Mussolini. . . .'

The sudden change for the better in the characters' fortunes removes, at least for the time being, their desperate uncertainty and thus the comedy associated with it. Instead, their new circumstances allow the personalitieis of Carmela and Paulina to reveal themselves in other ways. When, for example, they find themselves in the house of the mayor they had seen taken from the schoolroom and shot, the opportunity for love-making in comfort, offered by his bedroom and denied them for so long, emphasizes once more the deep feeling between them. On the other hand, it also draws attention to their differences. For example, Paulino is concerned only with the satisfaction of his sexual appetites, while Carmela, much more sensitive and considerate, is discomfited by the presence on the wall of the dead mayor's photograph, as well as by the fact that they are lying in his bed. Although there is a comic aspect to the spectacle of Paulino's burning desire and Carmela's scruples, the conflict is one which will now become much sharper.

The variety show is to be performed for the Nationalists, and Paulino has re-written their old script. From the outset Carmela expresses her reservations: 'You know what? This new number with the flag is vulgar. You should be ashamed of having written it.' Her love of Paulino does not mean that she is unaware of his shortcomings, a fact which she expresses very succinctly at this point: 'You're an angel on stage and a devil in bed. For anything else you are shit-scared.' Paulino's subsequent actions confirm her opinion that, at bottom, he is a man who, like Sancho Panza, is mainly concerned with himself.[8] In relation to the script and the show, Paulino's preoccupation is that it should succeed and that he and Carmela should continue to live without risk and in relative comfort. In this respect the episode in the dressing room where he tucks into food and sends Gustavete for wine is very revealing. Carmela, in contrast, voices her worries about the possible presence of the Polish prisoners at the performance: '. . . if they do bring the Poles to the theatre, this [script] is a bitch. . . How can they bring them if they are to be shot tomorrow?' Paulino's reaction is almost one of indifference: 'It might help distract them.' Carmela feels for one of the Polish soldiers' mother; Paulino points out that she will not know his fate. The episode ends with her calling him a brute. She cannot, however, deny the logic of the view he expresses slightly later: 'Wasn't surviving two years of war enough for you! . . . Remember the mayor and the school?. . . Get out on the road and see what's buried in the ditches!'

The revised version of the variety show constitutes the final third of the film. The preliminaries to the performance, true to the film's spirit as a whole, combine the comic with the serious, but in a new way which becomes more marked as events unfold. The comic note is struck in that both artistes are somewhat indisposed; Carmela has a period, Paulino a stomach upset, the result of eating a rabbit which Gustavete, writing on his slate, now confirms was a cat. Against this, the presence of the Polish prisoners greatly upsets Carmela, causing her to refuse to do the number with the flag. The comic moments are now placed in the context of a new and growing tension which, associated with the concert itself, strongly affects Carmela and Paulino. Comedy, indeed, placed in the context of Nationalist fervour and imminent executions, acquires a new edge, an element of desperation which gives it a considerable blackness.

The show consists of half a dozen 'turns', the first of which is Carmela's song about the horse, heard previously at the Republican concert. It has now been revamped for Nationalist propaganda purposes, allusions to the horse replaced by references to Spain: 'My Spain gallops and cuts the wind to build a monument to its brave Caudillo. My Spain is mad with joy because the day is drawing near to raise our arm in salute. . . .' In contrast to the original folk song, the words are both meaningless and absurd, but their reception by an ecstatic audience underlines its unthinking acceptance of what it wishes to believe. The third item consists of a poem, 'The Ballad of Castile in Arms', read by Paulino, in which a dreadful sentimentality goes hand in hand with a total lack of taste:

On the hill of the Angels, which angels guard,

prop' pieces so typical of the time, and is beautifully
played by Carmela, Paulino and Gustavete.[9] Paulino
plays a gay Republican doctor called Serafín Tocametoda
(Touchmeup) who is visited by a female patient, the
Spanish Republic, played by Carmela. Claiming that
she has been made pregnant by a Russian lover, played
by Gustavete, she invites the doctor to stick his ther-
mometer in, but he is forced to confess that it is broken.
The political appropriateness of the characters, the
crude yet spirited humour of the situation, and the
dialogue, together with Carmela and Paulino's timing
and delivery, create some delightful comic moments.
But then the comic mood begins to disappear. A mal-
functioning lighting system creates an eerie, flickering
effect. The Polish prisoners start shouting; Carmela
exposes her breast to the audience, insulting them
verbally too. Fighting breaks out between the Poles
and their guards. The Poles begin to sing defiantly;
Paulino tries to divert attention from Carmela with his
comic antics. The mounting tension of the sequence is
superbly orchestrated, the various actions underpinned
by the insistent drum beat on the soundtrack. None of
this, however, quite prepares us for what happens
next. A Nationalist officer suddenly shoots Carmela
through the head, and she falls to the floor slowly, to
the accompaniment of a drum beat and orchestral strings,
the shouting of the audience blocked out, her face and
the bullet-wound in close-up, illuminated by the white,
flickering light. It is an unexpected, incredible, stunning moment, a moment of true horror in which the
affection we have come to feel for this warm, compassionate, sensitive and attractive woman is, in an instant,
turned to tears. Perhaps the most moving moment of
all is when Gustavete, seen in close-up, suddenly calls
out in anguish, finding his voice for the first time when

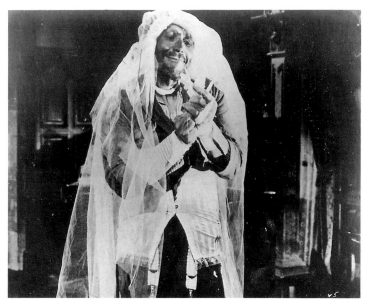

Scenes from *Viridiana* (Glenbuck Distributors)

Scenes from *The Exterminating Angel* (Contemporary Distr.)

Tristana (Artificial Eye)

Tristana (Artificial Eye)

Scenes from *The Hunt* (Glenbuck Distributors)

Raise Ravens (Gala Film Distributors)

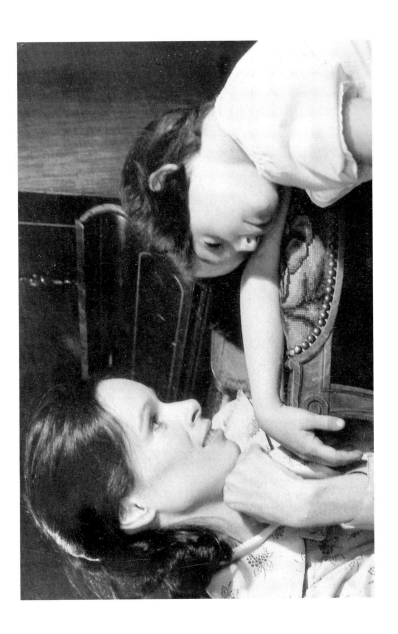

Raise Ravens (Gala Film Distributors)

Carmen (Curzon Film Distributors)

Carmen (Curzon Film Distributors)

Scenes from *Ay, Carmela!* (Glenbuck Distributors)

Spirit of the Beehive (Glenbuck Distributors)

Spirit of the Beehive (Glenbuck Distributors)

Scenes from *South* (Glenbuck Distributors)

Scenes from *Matador* (Metro Films)

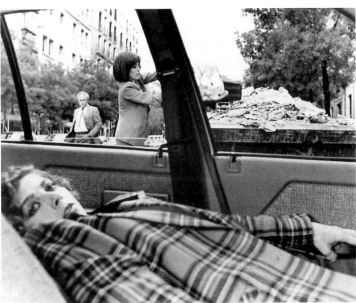

Women on the Edge of a Nervous Breakdown (Rank Film Distr.)

Scenes from *High Heels* (Rank Film Distributors)

Carmela cannot hear him. This, surely, is one of the most brilliant and accomplished sequences in the whole of Saura's film career; an incomparable moment when the comic suddenly becomes deeply tragic.

The film ends with a transition from the theatre to a vast, flat landscape and a great expanse of dark, lowering sky. The only figures to be seen are Paulino and Gustavete placing flowers on Carmela's grave before going on their way. By omitting the events immediately following her death, Saura allows us to imagine how much they must have grieved. The only words here are spoken by Gustavete — 'Come on, Paulino' — as he leads Paulino away, his arm around Paulino's shoulder in a gesture of solidarity and companionship. It is a simple, eloquent and immensely touching ending. As the two men walk away, the song 'Ay, Carmela!' is heard on the soundtrack, a lament to a truly remarkable woman. The ending of the film is, in a sense, tragic in the classical manner, for Carmela's death arouses the true tragic emotions of fear and pity. Her progessively heroic stand is one which inspires admiration and pity when such valour is destroyed. In addition, it evokes a sense of fear that such things can happen. There is also, perhaps, that sense of release of strong emotions which is catharsis. Beyond this, however, Carmela's fate stands for that of thousands of others who died for their beliefs in the Civil War. The final shot of the vast Spanish landscape is thus an appropriate setting in which the life of one individual, who is at the same time representative of many, can be placed.

Notes

1. From the dossier on *Ay, Carmela!*, Madrid, 1990, pp. 11–12.

2. See dossier, p. 10: 'La obra de teatro. Dificultades de la adaptación.' Sinisterra's play was staged in an English translation in 1992 by Loose Change Theatre Company at the Battersea Arts Centre, London.

3. Dossier, p. 11.

4. Dossier, p. 11. For the adaptation Saura had as his co-scriptwriter Rafael Azcona who had worked with him many times before but with whom he had broken in 1975 prior to the making of *Raise Ravens*. At that time Saura had regarded Azcona's misogyny as unsuited to the making of a film about women. In 1990 he attributed their disagreement to personality factors.

5. The song 'Ay, Carmela!', which begins and ends the film, was the favourite song of the Republican soldiers and of the International Brigade during the Civil War.

6. Alejandro Massó — see dossier, pp. 71–76 — makes many interesting and illuminating observations on the music used in the film, emphasizing in particular the efforts that were made to recreate the songs and the different kinds of musical accompaniment which would have been used in concerts and the like during the Civil War.

7. This 'serious' episode, its grimness heightened by the accompanying drum-beat, is clearly reminiscent of certain moments in *The Hunt*, but in reminding us of that film, *Ay, Carmela!*, suggests how far Saura has come in the intervening period in terms of his complete control of the art of film-making, including the juxtapositioning of contrasting elements.

8. The Don Quixote-Sancho Panza parallel had occurred previously in Buñuel's *Nazarín* where the idealistic priest has his down-to-earth counterpart in the prostitute who accompanies him on his journey along the roads of Spain. The relationship and journey of Carmela and Paulino has similar overtones.

9. A comparison may be made, on the Republican side, with Rafael Alberti's *Radio Sevilla*, written in 1936–7, in which great fun is obtained at the expense of the Nationalist general, Queipo de Llano.

The Spirit of the Beehive

The Spirit of the Beehive received its première in Madrid in October 1973 and has since proved to be one of the most haunting and mysterious films to come out of Spain, winning First Prize at the San Sebastian Film Festival in the year of its release. Previously, Erice had co-founded and written for the Spanish film magazine *Nuestro Cine* and had made no full-length feature films. An episode for which he was responsible in *Los desafíos (The Challenges)* in 1969 had attracted the attention of Elías Querejeta, the producer closely associated with Saura, and led him to consider Erice's idea for a film about Frankenstein monster. It appears that Erice's original intention had been to make a political allegory in which the monster returned to a concentration camp in Spain run by technocrats.[1] In the end he went in quite a different direction, and the monster itself proved to be the starting point for a film far more subtle and evocative than the original idea could possibly have inspired.

The direct influence on *The Spirit of the Beehive*, as far as the theme of the monster is concerned, was James Whale's *Frankenstein*, made by Universal Studios in 1931 with Boris Karloff as the monster. Set in a stark and gloomy Central European location, the outdoor sequences occur in a barren and rocky wasteland, the indoor sequences mainly in an old mill which Dr Frankenstein uses as his laboratory in his efforts to create a human being. The opening sequence is set in a graveyard and the film then builds steadily to the monster's first appearance, revealed to the audience in medium shot, close-up and then extreme close-up until his huge, pale, fearsome face fills the screen. Portrayed as a creature devoid of reason and any glimmer of human feeling, the monster embarks on a series of murders, beginning with the Dwarf, whose dead body is subsequently seen hanging on the wall like some gruesome trophy. Later in the film the monster is befriended by a little girl who takes his hand, inviting him to play and offering him a flower. Uncomprehending, the monster proceeds to drown her in the lake on whose bank they have met. This episode provoked such public distaste that it was later deleted from the film.[2] It was, however, part of this sequence — a still depicting the monster and the little girl kneeling beside the lake — which fascinated Erice and determined the direction his own film would take. *The Spirit of the Beehive* would not, after all, be the political allegory he originally had in mind. He would focus instead on the children of Spain of his own generation and the meaning of the monster for them.

The Spirit of the Beehive begins with a series of children's drawings alongside which the titles appear: drawings of a train, a mushroom, a house with a well, a cinema screen portraying a little girl and a monster, a girl leaping over a bonfire. These in fact are moments and locations which are important in the film and suggest reality filtered through the child's imagination. They have a fresh, fairy-tale quality which is reinforced by the accompanying music and then by a title which announces the beginning of the film proper: 'Once Upon a Time.' These words may also bring to mind the opening sequences of Buñuel's *Un Chien andalou* which begin with precisely the same words and then depicts a razor cutting a young woman's eyeball. Fairy tales, it is perhaps suggested, have their dark side and the child's mind and imagination their shadowy corners.

The next title, in the opening sequence — 'Somewhere in Castile, about 1940' — introduces a landscape which is far removed from any wonderland. An old lorry approaches along a road which cuts through a flat, drab landscape in which browns, whites, greys and dull greens predominate; and when it enters a village, the buildings are seen to be old, shabby and crumbling, suggestive of a country and a way of life that has not changed for hundreds of years. This is a village in the heart of Spain one year after the conclusion of the Civil War and the first year of the Franco dictatorship. It is no coincidence that there should be a marked similarity between the opening shots of *The Spirit of the Beehive* and Saura's *The Hunt*, for in both films the landscape of Castile, symbolic of the victories and defeats of Spain through the ages and always the seat of government, also becomes an image of the aftermath of the Civil War and of the poverty and hardship into which the Franco regime would plunge Spain for many years.[3] In the context of the drab and depressing buildings, the group of children who suddenly appear to greet the lorry and the arrival of a new film are therefore the new generation, the children of Spain, poised in 1940 on the brink of a time-warp which would see the reassertion of old, conservative, traditional values. The point is effectively made by means of the contrast between the eager youngsters, desperate to see the film, and the town crier who announces its arrival in a kind of ritual that has not changed for centuries.

The projection of the film to an excited audience in the run-down building which serves as a cinema introduces the theme of the monster, doing so in a way which makes it particularly relevant to the village audience, and thus to Spain in general. On screen a man addresses the public, informing them of what they are about to see: 'It is the story of Doctor Frankenstein . . . a scientist who tried to create a human being . . . forgetting that only God can do that. . . It is one of the strangest stories ever heard. . . It concerns the great mysteries of creation, life and death. . . .' Although the speaker is part of the film, he acquires here an extraordinary authenticity, as though he were addressing this Spanish audience, an effect heightened by the way in which his own voice is accompanied by their chatter. This being the case, his words assume a particular relevance for them, and by extension for the wider audience watching Erice's film, and it is not too much of an imaginative leap to substitute his opening words with, 'It is the story of General Franco. . . .' It is a parallel which is not made specific — how could it be in 1973? — but rather implied in a manner which is characteristic of the film as a whole. *The Spirit of the Beehive* contains two key images — the monster and the beehive — but neither can be tied too specifically to any given person or situation. Rather their relevance shifts as the film unfolds, but it is precisely this shifting of association which gives *The Spirit of the Beehive* its rich and deeply mysterious quality. Erice has spoken of its 'fundamentally lyrical structure.'[4] It is certainly a highly poetic film.

A new sequence introduces in close-up a man whose face and head are covered by a protective mask and who is engaged in some activity not initially revealed to us. Seen in isolation, the shot suggests a scientist and, in the context of what the film has been about so far, a kind of Dr Frankenstein at work. In reality, as the shot opens up, the man is seen to be occupied with his beehives and, in particular, with puffing smoke onto the bees to make them drowsy. But if the opening shot evokes Dr Frankenstein, at the end of the sequence, when the man turns away from the camera, presenting a great shape looming over the hive, the protective hood obliterating all human associations, he becomes a kind of monster. The man, we soon discover, is Fernando, the father of the two small girls, Ana and Isabel, who are the film's main characters, and he is engaged in the study of bees which has become his main interest in life. This being the case, how is it that he evokes the contradictory associations of Dr Frankenstein, the creator, and the monster, his creation, at one and the same time? It is a double image whose meaning becomes clear as the film unfolds. And what of the beehive? Close-ups of the bees in the hive suggest, clearly, a community, in particular an enclosed community, of which, on a human scale the village is an example. And in the sense that the bees are inert, deadened by the smoke applied to them, so the village and the community of Spain as a whole have been deadened, paralyzed, sapped of their energy by the War, of which the smoke of gun fire and burning buildings is but one manifestation.[5] By evoking both Dr Frankenstein and his monster, Fernando becomes an image for Franco, the instigator of the war, who is also a monster, and who, in the shattered wreck of his country, has, like Dr Frankenstein, produced a monster: not merely the men and women who are crippled physically but those whose lives, like the bees, are deadened and plunged into apathy.

A little later the parallel between Fernando and Dr Frankenstein is made again. On his way home Fernando

stops outside the cinema and looks at the poster advertising the film. Just afterwards, as he sits in his study,
the soundtrack of the film is heard over the shot of him
reading. The words are Dr Frankenstein's: 'Where would
we be if nobody tried to find out what lies beyond?
Have you never wanted to look beyond the clouds and
the stars, or to know what causes trees to bud, what
changes darkness into light. . . .?' The words are to do
with both his and mankind's restless search for knowledge. As we hear them, Fernando opens the window of
the room to reveal the distance and the sky beyond, the
mystery of the universe which is the object of man's
constant curiosity. In his own way Fernando is Dr
Frankenstein, his particular intellectual curiosity directed to the study of bees. In another sequence a
close-up of him in his study, earphones on his head,
reinforces the image, and we see Fernando poring over
his note-books late into the night. But there is another
point to consider. As Ana looks at a photograph album
later in the film, we see that Fernando, eleven years
previously, was a student at University, depicted here
in a photograph with the writer and philosopher, Miguel
de Unamuno, and the University was Salamanca, one
of Spain's leading educational establishments. Fernando
was an intellectual, like Dr Frankenstein, and just as
Frankenstein's pursuit of knowledge was constantly
blocked by the prejudice of others, so Fernando's career has been thwarted by war, diverted now into the
study of bees in a remote Spanish village in which there
is neither equipment nor stimulation. In this sense his
hopes and dreams have been deadened and the bees he
studies, dazed by smoke, are an image of him.[6]

Another parallel connects the beehive and Fernando's
house. An early close-up of the hive reveals its honeycomb or mesh pattern, which in turn is repeated in the

windows of the house in a variety of sequences. Indeed, in one particular shot, as Fernando sleeps in his study, a kind of mesh funnel inside which bees are crawling is seen inside the house, the pattern of the mesh echoed in the window immediately behind it. The image is one which suggests enclosure and imprisonment in a variety of ways. As the bees are confined to the cells and passageways of the hive, so Fernando's life is circumscribed by his circumstances. He is in effect imprisoned in a backwater, his intellectual gifts largely unrealized. To that extent his watch evokes the idea of time passing and people suspended in the endless monotony of unproductive and even meaningless lives. In addition, Fernando's marriage to Teresa, both of them students at university, seems to express the frustration of their hopes in general. Barely a word passes between them throughout the film. When she lies in bed at one point and he enters the bedroom late at night, she pretends to be asleep. At this point, his shadow looms large on the wall behind her, a menacing shape which evokes the monster. But it is not Fernando himself who is the monster in their marriage — rather their thwarted ambitions and economic hardship which cast a permanent shadow. If the prison image is suggested by means of the beehive, it is reinforced at the beginning of this sequence by the way in which the shadow of the head-rail of Teresa's bed is reflected on the wall like the bars of a cell.

While Fernando attempts to escape into the world of his bees, Teresa does so in a secret correspondence. When we first see her, she is writing a letter to someone with whom she had a relationship during the War and whom she has not seen since: 'Though I realize our happy hours together will never return . . . I ask God to grant me the joy of being with you again. I have prayed

for this ever since we parted during the War. . . .'
Although we are given no specific information, it seems
likely that the person to whom she writes is a Republican, possibly a friend or colleague of Fernando, who is
now either imprisoned or an exile.[7] Whether or not he
is still alive or whether he writes to her remains unclear. What is very evident is that for Teresa the 'affair',
however real or insubstantial, is an escape from the
numbing monotony of her everyday life to which the
conclusion of the letter refers: '. . . when I look around
for things that are gone . . . the destruction of so many
things, the creation of so much misery . . . I feel we
have also lost our perception of the essence of life. . . .'
The illusory nature of experience is effectively suggested by the golden light that comes through the
window, but simultaneously the honeycomb pattern of
the glass is a reminder of enclosure and imprisonment
and therefore of the fact that for Teresa there is no
escape from her bleak surroundings. Indeed, as she
cycles to the railway station to post the letter, it is the
reality of the dull, monotonous landscape and the road
which leads nowhere which impose themselves. Furthermore, if the soldiers on the train remind Teresa of
her lover, the train itself, as it leaves the station, reminds us of other, distant places and of how cut off,
marooned in their prison world the people of the village are.[8]

If the early part of *The Spirit of the Beehive* focuses on
Fernando and Teresa, it is their children, Ana and
Isabel, who later become the centre of attention. Ana, in
particular, has been greatly impressed by the monster
and later that night questions Isabel about it. Two
questions in particular preoccupy her: 'Why did the
monster kill the girl and why did they kill him?' Isabel
replies that no one died in the film because 'in films

everything is untrue', but suggests to Ana that the monster exists outside the film, in the real world; that he is in fact a spirit who dwells in the bodies of other people; and that if Ana is a friend of his she can talk to him at any time by closing her eyes and calling out, 'I'm Ana.' The crucial point here is Isabel's suggestion that the monster exists outside the film in multiple forms. It immediately transforms the world in which Ana is growing up into a much more mysterious, intriguing and even frightening place than it already is. As for Erice, it allows him both to explore in a highly evocative way the mind and imagination of an impressionable child, and to broaden the range of reference of the monster associations in a way which may not otherwise have been possible.

While in one sense *The Spirit of the Beehive* is about intellectual curiosity, it is in another about Ana's curiosity in relation to her expanding world in all its various manifestations.[9] In this respect Ana's open, inquiring expression (she is played by Ana Torrent who two years later would appear in *Raise Ravens*) suggests the blank page or 'tabula rasa' commented on previously. As Ana and Isabel run home from the cinema, we see them shouting and screaming, doubtless reliving the experience of the film. As they lie in bed, talking in hushed tones, Isabel's explanation of the monster becomes the sound of Fernando's heavy footsteps pacing in his study, as if the monster were coming up the stairs. Later, again in bed, they are using their hands to throw shadows on the wall when they hear Fernando approaching. They react with awe and fear, quickly extinguishing the candle. For the children, the father is the monster, but in what sense? Isabel's definition, accepted by Ana, of the monster as a spirit who inhabits other bodies is perfectly comprehensible here. In the course of the film, with the one exception of the mush-room sequence, Fernando is a solitary, silent presence, often dressed in his beekeeper's clothes, often pacing his study at night, rarely in the company of his wife or children. For the children, then, he is indeed a strange, mysterious and alien being. For the spectator of the film there are other associations too. As we have seen, the relationship of Fernando and Teresa is one that is marked by its lack of communication, and the family unit could hardly be termed ideal. If, then, it was Franco's intention to promote the idea of the perfect family, just as Dr Frankenstein sought to create the perfect man, the reality was flawed indeed, the one as badly botched as the other.[10]

Throughout the second half of the film the theme of the child growing up and of its curiosity, wonder and even terror in the face of new experiences is sensitively explored. The village school, centre of the children's formative years, stimulates their intellectual curiosity. At one point one of the pupils reads a poem:

> No more anger or disdain,
> Nevermore a fear of change.
> Just an ever-present thirst
> For something that destroys me.
> Stream of life, where are you bound?
> Air, I need more air!
> What is in the murky depths
> That makes you tremble and whisper?
> I see what a blind man sees
> When he stares at the sun.
> I shall sink into the depths
> And the waves won't let me return.

The allusions to 'an ever-present thirst', the 'stream of

life' and to seeing 'what a blind man sees' seem to refer
to a curiosity and an instinctive desire to penetrate the
mysteries of the world which equate the children with
Dr Frankenstein. As in his case, the experience may
well bring dangers with it. Their relevance to Ana is
suggested here not only by the fact that she is one of the
class listening to the poem but that she silently mouths
its words.[11] Prior to this the learning experience is also
seen in the sequence where Fernando teaches his daughters to distinguish between harmless and harmful
mushrooms. It is a sequence full of rich and often
ambiguous associations. The mountain beyond the village where mushrooms grow in profusion engages
Ana's attention, suggestive, like the train, of a world
beyond the village as yet unknown to her. It is a source
of fascination and mystery as great as that embodied in
the questions which haunt her: 'Why did the monster
kill the girl and why did they kill him?' In addition,
when they discover a large, poisonous mushroom,
described by Fernando as 'a real devil', Ana's voice is
hushed and full of awe before this other kind of monster. Fernando's words — 'See the colour of its cap,
look at its black stem. Don't ever forget it. It's the most
poisonous.' — as well as the mushroom's shape, have
a clear phallic association of which the six-year old
child would as yet be unaware but which may point,
nevertheless, to sexual fears and fascinations that lie
ahead. For the moment, however, the mushroom embodies a much more general threat, an evil to be
recognized in a bewildering world and, as Fernando
demonstrates, to be stamped upon. For him, as opposed to the children, the mushroom no doubt suggests
many other things, not least the poisonous growth of
fascism which has destroyed his own life.

A second episode in the schoolroom presents yet

another, if somewhat comic, monster in the shape of
the cardboard cut-out of a man without a heart, lungs,
stomach or eyes. When the teacher asks the class 'Who
left Don José like that?' and they reply, 'You did, miss!',
she becomes a kind of Dr Frankenstein of the class-
room, and the lesson which follows, in which the children
attempt to put the organs in the right place, a humor-
ous variation on 'a scientist who tried to create a human
being.' For them, nevertheless, this is a serious business into which they enter with enviable enthusiasm,
and when at the end Ana is asked to give him eyes, she
looks up at the completed figure with an expression of
awe.[12]

The progression of monsters, from father to mushroom to cardboard cut-out, leads finally to the fugitive
in the abandoned house. Immediately after the 'anatomy'
lesson, Isabel had suggested to Ana that the monster
lives in the old house, a conviction which seems confirmed when Ana goes to the house alone and discovers
a footprint much larger than her own. Later still Isabel
plays a trick on her by pretending to be dead, leading
Ana to believe the monster has killed her, just as he did
the child in the film. When Ana returns after seeking
help and finds her sister's body gone, her confusion
becomes terror when she hears footsteps behind her
and a gloved hand covers her face. A smiling Isabel
reveals the source of the trick, but the incident also
reveals the impressionable mind of the child and the
way in which the imagination so easily transforms
reality. By the time she encounters the fugitive, she is
seeing monsters everywhere.

The fugitive is, in all probability, a Republican on the
run, perhaps escaped from a Nationalist prison, and
his coat and gun remind us of the War.[13] For Ana, on
the other hand, he is clearly the being which the spirit

of the monster inhabits when he goes out at night. When she gives him an apple, her gesture echoes that of the child in the Frankenstein film when she offers the monster a flower; a gesture of friendship and of generosity and, perhaps, an echo of the ending of Buñuel's *Nazarín* when, in an act of pure compassion, a woman offers some fruit to a suffering human being. The apple also suggests the innocence of the child and, although she is not directly to blame, the fugitive's subsequent betrayal. At all events, there is between the man and the child a bond of friendship, reinforced by the food and the clothes she brings him later and heightened by their lack of conversation. When he performs a conjuring trick with her father's watch, making it disappear, their mutual smile points to the growing bond between them.

If Ana befriends the 'monster', others destroy him. Unknown to her, the police have tracked him down and shot him during the night. In terms of his death at the hands of others, the Frankenstein film and reality coincide, and it is therefore no coincidence that the corpse of the fugitive is laid out in the cinema, before the very screen on which the monster appeared. But for Ana herself, the question remains: who is the monster, who the victim? Returning to the old house, she finds her friend gone and blood on the floor. When her father enters, he becomes for her the murderer, and the question 'why did they kill him?' fills her imagination. Upset and confused, she runs off, ignoring her father's order to come back, and for several days and nights cannot be found. Seeking to come to terms with the death of her friend and the reason for it, she kneels by a pool and, transforming reality into the world of imagination, sees Frankenstein's monster approach and kneel beside her in a repeat of the scene in the film. He touches her arm and shoulder, she looks at him with bated breath, but, in contrast to the film, he does not kill her. Eventually found by a search party, Ana is taken home, traumatized by her experience.

These scenes reveal in the most haunting and evocative way Ana's attempt to make sense of the terrible events which have suddenly overtaken her. Refusing to believe that the 'monster' fugitive, is bad, she conjures him up in the scene by the pool — this time in his original form — to prove to herself that he is good and will not harm her.[14] If others, in particular her father, have killed him, it follows that they are the bad ones and that her question, 'why did they kill him?' can now be answered. Furthermore, if the monster is a spirit, he cannot really die but can be invoked by those who are his friends. In a wonderfully mysterious last sequence Ana opens her window at night, recalling her sister's words: 'If you're a friend of his you can talk to him at any time. You shut your eyes and you can say to him: "It's Ana!" ' The final shot of the film is of Ana closing her eyes, expressing an innocence that is full of hope in a world in which there is little sign of hope. The killing of the fugitive, recalling the carnage of Saura's *The Hunt*, embodies the Spain of the Civil War, bloody, vindictive and full of hate. Ana's triumph over that suggests, in a quite uplifting way, that the ultimate future of Spain lies with its children.

Notes

1. On the background see John Hopewell, *Out of the Past . . .*, pp. 203–4.

2. For a discussion of the various Frankenstein films, including James Whale's, see Carlos Clarens, *Horror Movies: An Illustrated Survey*, London: Secker and Warburg, 1967, pp. 80–88.

3. John Hopewell, *Out of the Past . . .*, p. 207, suggests that 'Somewhere in Castile, about 1940' is an echo of the beginning of Cervantes's *Don Quixote*: 'In a place in La Mancha, whose name I do not wish to recall. . .' As in the Cervantes story, a particular place in the heartland of Spain becomes an image or a symbol for Spain as a whole.

4. See Pablo López, 'Las mejores películas de la historia del cine: *El espíritu de la colmena*', *Fotogramas*, no. 1689, September 1983, pp. 45–52.

5. Virginia Higginbotham, *Spanish Film Under Franco*, p. 117, makes the point that the windows of the house are an image that equates the monotonous life of its inhabitants with that of the bees in Fernando's hives.

6. In the published script of the film, Madrid: Ediciones Elías Querejeta, 1976, p. 144, Erice himself observes that there were many 'defeated men who, no matter which side they fought on, lived the war out without any clear idea of the reasons for their behaviour, acting simply to survive.' Fernando is an example of what Erice describes as 'the emptiness of Spaniards who fought in the war.'

7. On this point see John Hopewell, *Out of the Past . . .*, p. 207 and Vicente Molina Foix, 'La Guerra detrás de la ventana', *Revista de Occidente*, no. 53, October 1985.

8. At another point in the film the train is seen thundering past, dwarfing Ana and Isabel. It becomes, therefore, another 'monster', one of many in their lives and also an embodiment of how huge and threatening the world must seem to children in the process of growing up.

9. See Peter Evans, *El Espíritu de la Colmena*: The Monster, the Place of the Father, and Growing Up in the Dictatorship', *Vida Hispánica*, Autumn 1982, vol. XXXI, no. 3; and E.C. Riley, 'The Story of Ana in *El espíritu de la colmena*', *Bulletin of Hispanic Studies*, LXI, 1984, p. 494.

10. The same is true, of course, of the respective families referred to or seen in *The Hunt* and *Raise Ravens*.

11. The poem is by the Galician poet, Rosalía de Castro and was originally written in Galician. In the film it is recited in Castilian Spanish, the only language permitted under the dictatorship.

12. See John Hopewell, *Out of the Past* . . ., p. 204.

13. Virginia Higginbotham, *Spanish Film Under Franco*, p. 119, suggests: 'For the villagers, the wounded man is not Frankenstein but a maquis, of whom there were over fifty thousand at the close of the Civil War. To them he is a criminal and they kill him.'

14. John Hopewell, *Out of the Past* . . ., p. 208, takes a quite different line, suggesting that she expects the monster to kill her.

The South

The South was completed in 1983, ten years after *The Spirit of the Beehive*. Erice's intention was to make an entirely different kind of film, something which stemmed from his theoretical education in modernist film-making.[1] That he did not do so was due to a variety of reasons, including his own timidity, but perhaps the most important fact was the pressure placed on him to make another film in the style of *The Spirit of the Beehive*. *The South* was conceived, as Erice has stated himself, for 'major distribution channels.'[2] The producer was Elías Querejeta once more, but on this occasion things did not go smoothly and, when financial problems arose, Querejeta stopped filming before the project, as Erice had planned it, was completed.[3] As a result, the existing version of the film falls short of Erice's original intentions, and his co-scriptwriter, Angel Fernández Santos has described what was omitted from the script.[4] Even so, the version we have is a coherent piece of work, of sufficient quality to have impressed the critics when it was shown at the Cannes Film Festival in 1983 and to have made its mark subsequently in many countries.

Erice's love of Hollywood, already evident in the prominence of James Whale's *Frankenstein* in *The Spirit of the Beehive*, is revealed in this second film by the influence of Alfred Hitchcock's *Shadow of a Doubt*. Referred to in *The South* as a forthcoming attraction at the Arcadia cinema, Hitchcock's film is concerned with the fascination of a young girl, Charlie, for her Uncle Charlie, and the way in which, because of their close relationship, she transforms him into a surrogate father, a dashing adventurer and ideal lover with whom she seems to have a telepathic understanding. By the end of the film, however, Uncle Charlie is exposed as a murderer who lives off what he steals from the widows he kills, and Charlie herself, having discovered the truth about him, also discovers herself. In an interview about the influences on *The South*, Erice himself mentioned Hitchcock only once, without reference to any specific film, and alluded in particular to Ray's *Rebel Without a Cause* (1955) in which the relationship between parents and children is of key importance. There can be no doubt, however, given the many points of contact between *The South* and *Shadow of a Doubt*, that the latter played a more important role. In Erice's film there are also clues to literary influences: a cigar-box bears the name *Romeo and Juliet*; at the end of the film the protagonist, Estrella, reads *Wuthering Heights*; and earlier Estrella's mother is reading *Tess of the D'Urbervilles*. All three works are concerned with deeply felt love relationships, the idea of 'star-cross'd lovers', the supernatural in one way or another and with mystery; all elements central to *The South*. In a more general sense, as Peter Evans and Robin Fiddian have pointed out, Erice's film owes something to the Hollywood tradition of the 'Woman's Picture' such as *Stella Dallas* (1925) and *An Unmarried Woman* (1978), the genre of melodrama such as Hitchcock's *Rebecca* (1940) and film noir thrillers such as *Laura* (1944) and *The Woman in the Window* (1944).[5]

The South begins with a wonderfully breathless, tense and mysterious sequence which is reminiscent of the opening to *Raise Ravens*. The camera reveals a darkened bedroom in which the fifteen-year old Estrella awakens to a dog barking and voices calling out. A woman's voice shouts 'Agustín', footsteps are heard on the stairs, and then an exchange between two women:

> 'Casilda!'
> 'What is it, señora?'
> 'My husband's not here.'

Just afterwards a woman speaks on the telephone: 'Is that the hospital? May I speak to Dr Arenas? It's his wife.'

The other woman informs her that Estrella's bicycle has disappeared, and we gather from the remainder of the telephone conversation that Dr Arenas has not been at the hospital all night. After this flurry of activity, the second half of the sequence has an altogether calmer rhythm. To a cello accompaniment on the soundtrack, the camera focuses in close-up on Estrella's hands which are closed over an object she has taken from beneath her pillow. Opening slowly, like the petals of a flower, they reveal a small black container from which she takes a pendulum — a small weight on the end of a length of chain. A voice-over is heard: the voice of Estrella in later life commenting on the events she experienced at the age of fifteen and which we have just seen: 'That morning, when I found his pendulum beneath my pillow, I knew things were different. That this time he wasn't coming back.'

For the cinema audience this opening poses all kinds of questions: who are these people and what precisely is happening? By its conclusion we also become aware that the sequence involves two perspectives or time-scales, for what initially seems to be the present is seen to be the past revealed in flash-back, the girl in the bedroom the younger form of the woman whose voice we actually hear. The beginning of the film is thus a kind of guessing game, a mystery, that acts as a prelude to the film as a whole, for, as we shall see, its essence is a search for the truth, the unravelling of a past which is clouded in mystery.

The second sequence takes us even further back in time, some fifteen years earlier, to the circumstances surrounding Estrella's birth and the choice of her name. The older Estrella's voice is again heard and from now on becomes a frequent commentator on earlier events. At this particular point the camera shows us her father, Agustín, holding the pendulum over his wife's swollen abdomen, 'divining' that the child is a girl he will call Estrella, while the voice-over observes: 'They said my father had guessed I'd be a girl. That's the first thing I remember. A powerful image which, in truth, I invented.' These words suggest that the picture which Estrella constructs of her father is more fanciful than true, an idea which this short sequence illustrates. The shot of the father holding the pendulum over his wife and predicting the sex of the unborn child suggests a magical, mysterious power, while the golden light which illuminates the two figures, reminiscent of a painting by Vermeer, points to the idealized vision his daughter will later have of him.[6] It is precisely this relationship on which the early part of the film concentrates.

The image of Agustín as a man of mystery, a worker of miracles, is filled out in a variety of ways as the film unfolds. Estrella's inquiries about her father's secret activities in the upper room of the house draw from her mother Julia replies which add to his aura of fascination. She refers, in particular, to Augustín's powers and, when Estrella asks about their source, replies enigmatically: '... he just has them ... he was born with them.' In another sequence Agustín is seen teaching Estrella to use the pendulum, initiating her into the powers she believes him to have. It is another of those beautifully lit moments in which Agustín's calm and soothing voice, the cello accompaniment and the lighting itself evoke not only his power over the pendulum but also the spell he casts over his daughter. Another scene reveals him helping some local farmers to 'divine' water, on this occasion assisted by Estrella herself, while the voice-over observes: 'My father could do things other people regarded as miracles. But to me, his own daughter, those things seemed normal. . . .'

In addition, Estrella fashions a highly romantic image of her father's past, constructed from a minimum of actual information. Her mother tells her, for example, that Agustín is from the south of Spain, where it hardly ever snows; that his relationship with his father was not good; that he left when he was young and never wanted to go back. The story is sufficiently bare to allow the child to embroider it in her imagination, and when the voice-over of the older Estrella informs us: 'My father's origins were always a mystery to me,' the double meaning of 'mystery' as 'puzzle' on the one hand and 'fascination' on the other is highly significant. Indeed, the older woman admits to the fantasy: 'That story was always ripe for fantasy. I filled it with images I carried everywhere. Ignoring what the real distance was, I located it across the map. Somewhere in the South, with palm-trees in the background. . . .' The idealized, glamorous and somewhat romantic nature of Estrella's vision of her father's homeland is embodied in her collection of postcards and photographs of such places as Seville, with its colourful vegetation, beautiful patios, slender Moorish columns, splashing fountains and brightly costumed flamenco dancers.[7] If for the young Estrella her father is a figure of mystery in the present, he is also one in relation to the past. If he lacks a past, Estrella invents it.[8]

The arrival from the South of Agustín's mother and Milagros, his former wet-nurse, fills out the picture but in a way which, for Estrella, merely adds to his mystery. Sharing a room with Estrella, the warm, kindly and talkative Milagros confirms the rift between Agustín and his father and adds some important details. During the years of the Republic, she observes, Agustín was one of 'the good men' and his father one of 'the bad men', but after the Civil War and Franco's victory Agustín was one of 'the bad men,' 'a demon,' his father one of 'the good men,' 'a saint.' Her story is, however, short on specifics and raises in Estrella's mind more questions than it answers: in what sense was her father a good man? Why did he become a demon? The allusions to good and bad, saint and demon, place her father's story in the context of fairy tale and myth, investing it with precisely the kind of glamour on which the mind of a child feeds. By the time the women return to the south, Estrella's image of Agustín is, if anything, even further removed from reality.

The true nature of that reality is suggested to us early on. A brief sequence showing Estrella and her parents on a train is accompanied by the voice-over: 'I grew up always on the move. . . He [my father] was looking for a steady job. He found it in the North, in a walled city, by a river. We lived outside, in a rented house, "The Seagull." Built in no-man's land, between the country and the city, by a road my father used to call "The Frontier." ' In contrast to the idealized image fashioned by Estrella, the reality of her father's life is very different: a constant search for permanent employment, a succession of train journeys, the sense of a family uprooted. And even when Agustín finds work in the North, there is, in the circumstances of his life, a strong suggestion of his not belonging there, of isolation and alienation in a no-man's land by a road on the edge of somewhere where the sign of the seagull on the roof of the house points always to the South. As well as this, the evidence of the film itself is that the marriage of Agustín and Julia is less than entirely happy. Like the husband and wife of *The Spirit of the Beehive*, they rarely speak. Indeed, there is a parallel between Agustín and Fernando in the way in which both men isolate themselves in their study. As for Julia, she spends her time engaged in a series of purely domestic tasks: sewing, watering flowers, varnishing woodwork. The house with its different rooms with the husband and wife in different parts of it, separated by walls and floors, becomes an image of their increasing lack of communication and of the prison which their marriage has become. The magic with which Estrella associates her father is notable in his married life only by its absence.

If the early part of *The South* focuses on the child's false image of her father, the remainder of the film portrays its slow disintegration. It begins, significantly, with Estrella's first communion. It is, in a sense, the end of childhood, an initiation into the first stages of adulthood which marks, quite apart from the religious significance of the ritual itself, a loss of innocence and, as Peter Evans and Robbin Fiddian have observed, 'entry into the imperfect world of human relations.'[9] The preparations, the event itself and the party which follows present Estrella as a bride in white, an image which, apart from its suggestions of purity and spirituality, points to a new beginning. When Estrella dances a *pasodoble* with her father, possibly the first time she has danced with him, she seems already on the threshold of becoming a young woman.[10] Indeed, her delight when, against the predictions of Julia, he is present at her first Communion is soon transformed into confusion and uncertainty.[11]

The process begins when, looking through the contents of a drawer, Estrella discovers some sketches of a woman's face with the name 'Irene Ríos' written beneath it. The voice-over underlines the importance of this moment: 'I can't remember exactly, but I think it was about that time when I discovered there was another woman in my father's thoughts. . . .' It is a discovery which, prompting a series of questions in her own mind and reassuring her of her mother's ignorance on the matter, leads her to probe her father's past and in so doing to expose secrets hitherto unknown. The second half of *The South* is concerned with the discovery of his true identity, with Estrella's growing knowledge of her father's past and, in conjunction with it, her increasing knowledge of herself.

Seeing her father's motorcycle outside the town's cinema, Estrella discovers that the film, which Agustín is evidently watching, is *Flower in the Shadow* and its star Irene Ríos, whose photograph is prominently displayed. Estrella then waits for him to emerge, watches him go into the Café Oriental, and shortly afterwards surprises him as he writes a letter. Unable to enter the cinema on account of her age, Estrella does not see the film, nor does she know that the letter is for Irene Ríos. The latter is, indeed, confirmed by the voice-over, 'All I knew was that he was writing what I thought was a letter.' The young Estrella is intelligent enough to be suspicious, and her suspicions are soon confirmed by raised voices at home which point to another woman in Agustín's life. If she once saw her father as a magical and mysterious being, she now begins to see him dif-

ferently and, more significantly, to feel differently towards him. As the voice-over suggests: 'I began to feel
differently about my father. It was as if I'd opened my
eyes . . . and realized how little I knew him.'

Agustín is in reality a man whose capacity for fantasy is in its own way as great as his daughter's. He is,
on the one hand, a doctor at the hospital in the town;
someone who deals with hard fact and scientific evidence. On the other, he is a dreamer whose relationship
with Irene Ríos in the South continues to haunt him
and to appear more desirable on account of his own
disintegrating marriage. It is no coincidence that the
cinema — the archetypal source of illusion — where
Agustín sees one of Irene Ríos's films, should become
the focus and the symbol of his escape into fantasy. The
name of the cinema, 'Arcadia', is itself evocative of a
world of dreams. Above the name, moreover, is a great
fanlight in the shape of a fan whose coloured glass,
suggesting green leaves and flowers mixed in with
blue and yellow, creates a visual link with Estrella's
postcards and photographs of the South, therefore
telling us where her father's dreams lie. Inside the
cinema Agustín watches on screen a fiction which in
many ways is a re-enactment of his own relationship
with Irene Ríos. The sequence we see begins with her
singing 'Blue Moon', whose words 'without a dream in
my heart, without a love of my own' match precisely
Agustín's situation.[12] There follows a scene of bitter
recrimination between the woman played in the film
by Irene and a former lover who finally shoots her and,
as she lies dying, tells her, 'You were singing our song.
We could have been so happy. . . .' They are words
which, despite the melodramatic nature of the on-
screen events, are keenly felt by Agustín as he watches
a film in which the woman he loved and left behind

plays a woman killed by a man who cannot forget her. The man's final anguished outburst becomes a close-up of Agustín, his eyes closed, his expression full of pain.

The letter which he writes to Irene in the Café Oriental is the first step in an attempt to resurrect their relationship and transform dream into reality. A slightly later sequence in the same café reveals her reply, which destroys that dream, confronting it with harsh truth. In a tone which is fairly brutal, Irene makes a decisive break with him, resolving to put the past behind her. She informs Agustín that she has turned her back on the cinema and that the *femme fatale* he wrote to has now become 'the late Irene Ríos.' The letter suggests that she has abandoned the world of illusion, the cinema, and that the *femme fatale* she has played on screen and around which Agustín has fashioned his own illusion, is no more. In suggesting that she has 'finally grown up', she prescribes a course which he must also accept, however difficult that might be. Significantly, the beginning of the disintegration of Agustín's world is accompanied in the background by the jarring notes of a piano being tuned.

The last third of *The South* focuses on Estrella's growing up, her movement away from her father and the increasing meaninglessness of his own life. Initially, as far as she is concerned, the discovery of another woman in his life inspires feelings of jealousy, and in the quiet of her bedroom she burns the leaflet with its portrait of Irene Ríos which she had obtained from the cinema. In conjunction with this, a boy, Carioco, shows an interest in Estrella, telephoning her, and declaring his love for her by painting 'I love you' on walls. At home she becomes increasing aware of, and disturbed by, the growing rift between her parents. As she sits on a swing in the garden and watches her father restlessly pacing in his upstairs room, the harsh creaking of the swing encapsulates family discord, as well as her own confused feelings. Weary of the bad atmosphere, she protests at one point by hiding under her bed, making her parents believe she has left home. Later, her desire to run away from home is accompanied by a pessimism surprising in one still so young: 'I was getting used to being on my own and not bothering about happiness.'

As for Agustín, his life is slowly falling apart. In this respect, his daughter's name is significant. In deciding to call her Estrella ('star') he doubtless wished to give her some of that magic and mystery with which he is associated. Agustín brings to mind another father: King Basilio in Calderón's famous seventeenth-century play, *Life is a Dream*, who boasts of his ability to read the stars and attempts to predict his child's future. It is a play in which the star as an image — the King's niece is also called Estrella — is important in ways which find significant echoes in *The South*. Initially, Estrella is very much a star in Agustín's life, filling it with light and beauty. When he loses touch with another kind of star, Irene Ríos, Estrella eclipses her to a large extent. Later, of course, when she grows up and circumstances change, she becomes a star which fades from her father's heaven.[13] In addition, as events unfold, the image of the star becomes more clearly linked to the notion of fate, for in their different ways Estrella and Irene Ríos are the stars which greatly influence Agustín's death, the one by growing away from him, the other by ending their relationship. In a particularly memorable sequence, Estrella is seen holding a skein of bright red wool which her mother winds into a ball. The episode is a clear echo of the scene in Lorca's *Blood Wedding* in which three girls, symbolic of the Fates, unwind red wool, an image of the thread of life. But what is especially striking in the film is the way in which the wool, and by implication, Agustín's life, is literally in the hands of Estrella and her mother. And when Estrella, aware of the rift between her parents, hurls the wool to the floor, its blood-red colour is already a prophecy of Agustín's death. It is no coincidence, therefore, that the voice-over should refer to his situation as 'something familiar and inevitable.'

The most crucial episode occurs in the dining room of The Grand Hotel, to which Agustín has unexpectedly invited Estrella for lunch. There have been several occasions prior to this when his behaviour has upset her; occasions on which he has left home only to return, sometimes at dawn, or when she has seen him drunk in the street. The lunch is a painful attempt on Agustín's part to bring about a reconciliation with a daughter he knows is growing up and away from him. As he puts it himself, 'I wanted to make peace.' In almost every way the occasion proves to be a disaster. It is the fifteen year-old Estrella who is by far the more communicative and who seeks the answers to questions which only he can give, in particular concerning Irene Ríos. Instead, she encounters a defensive wall, a man who, instead of admitting the truth to the daughter he loves, retreats into his shell and reveals almost nothing. Indeed, when Agustín leaves the table to wash his face, eager to escape a situation which he finds very difficult, he returns to find Estrella ready to depart and evidently disappointed. It is at this moment that the *pasodoble* to which Agustín and Estrella danced at her First Communion is heard from a wedding reception in the room next door and which now, some years later, becomes even more significant. As Estrella looks at the bride through the glass, she sees herself as she was at her

First Communion. The bride, moreover, dances with her husband as Estrella did with her father. But the wedding marks for the bride a break with her past. As the *pasodoble* is heard again, another, much more crucial break is announced. Estrella has met her father, talked to him and discovered there is little common ground. As she leaves the dining room, her waving goodbye is sadly prophetic. She will never see him again.

Agustín shoots himself on a river bank, as lonely in death as he was in life, while back at the house the dog barks and Julia's voice calls 'Agustín!' The action of the film has come full circle, the mystery of its opening sequence now explained. The overwhelming feeling of this episode is one of isolation, of individuals in a family who have lost touch with each other. Agustín's body lies on the river bank, so far unnoticed. Julia's voice calls out from the house but finds no response. Estrella sits in her room staring at the pendulum. As in the case of *The Spirit of the Beehive*, this is a family in which there is only a sense of disintegration, effectively suggested by the personal effects laid out by Agustín before his suicide; wallet, cigarette-case, watch, pen, key, coins, the remaining debris of his life. Between Estrella and Julia there is little evidence of the genuine coming-together that the death of a father and husband might suggest. A shot of Estrella looking sadly from an upstairs window is a more accurate measure of the prevailing mood.

The film ends with Estrella's departure for the South at the invitation of Milagros. In one way it is an optimistic ending, for the photographs and colourful cover of the book she packs in her case suggest a departure from the gloom, physical and spiritual, of the North. But the book also contains a telephone number she had found with her father's belongings, a number which he had rung on the last night of his life and which is in all probability Irene Ríos's. In the sense that this points to the possible discovery of further truths, to a further exploration, the ending of the film is suitably enigmatic.

As well as concerning itself with one particular family, *The South* is also concerned, like so many of the films of the dictatorship, with the family of Spain. The polarities of the North and the South suggest the theme of the nation divided, while Agustín's dispute with his father and his virtual exile from the South is but one particular example of many such quarrels and many such exiles.[14] In addition, Agustín's house, set in a kind of no-man's land, evokes both the sense of isolation and the lack of direction in the lives of so many families after the Civil War. This feeling is intensified by our awareness of the divisions and ruptures within Agustín's household where individuals seem to live their lives in separate parts of the house and are emotionally and spiritually ever more distant from each other. Set in 1957, eighteen years into the dictatorship and seventeen years after the events portrayed in *The Spirit of the Beehive*, *The South* is a worthy counterpart to the earlier film both in its indictment of the dictatorship itself and in its wonderfully suggestive, mysterious and poetic evocation of particular lives.

Notes

1. See an interview with Vicente Molina Foix, 'Victor Erice: El cine de los supervivientes', *Mayo*, no. 12, September 1983.

2. John Hopewell, *Out of the Past* . . ., p. 210.

3. See Peter Evans and Robin Fiddian, 'Victor Erice's *El Sur*: A Narrative of Star-Cross'd Lovers', *Bulletin of Hispanic Studies*, LXIV, 1987, p. 127.

4. '33 preguntas eruditas sobre El Sur', *Casablanca*, nos. 31–32, July–August 1983, pp. 55–58.

5. Peter Evans and Robin Fiddian, 'Victor Erice's *El Sur* . . . .', pp. 127, 135.

6. Lighting effects of a similar kind are equally evident in *The Spirit of the Beehive*, notably when light pours in through the honeycomb windows of the house. Prior to the making of this film, Erice had shown his camera-man, Luis Cuadrado, copies of paintings by Vermeer and Rembrandt.

7. John Hopewell, *Out of the Past* . . ., p. 213, suggests that for Estrella the South is a kind of 'earthly paradise' and that her 'view of Agustín's past conforms to religious myth'.

8. Peter Evans and Robin Fiddian, 'Victor Erice's *El Sur* . . .', p. 130, note: 'The image she formed of her father . . . is consequently an idealized image rooted in nostalgia, distortion and even fantasy'.

9. Peter Evans and Robin Fiddian, 'Victor Erice's *El Sur* . . .', p. 130.

10. The tune which is being played is called 'En el mundo' ('In the World'), suggestive enough of Estrella on the threshold of a new stage of life.

11. The relationship between Estrella and her father corre-
    sponds very largely to father-daughter relationships
    described by Freud in *On Sexuality. Three Essays on the
    Theory of Sexuality and Other Works*, trans. James Strachey
    and ed. Angela Richards, Harmondsworth: Penguin,
    1977. See in particular the essay 'Family Romances';
    and 'Femininity', in *New Introductory Lectures on Psy-
    choanalysis*, trans. James Strachey and Angela Richards.
    Harmondsworth: Penguin, pp. 145–169.

12. Peter Evans and Robin Fiddian, 'Victor Erice's *El Sur
    ...*', note that 'Blue Moon' featured in Douglas Sirk's
    film, *There's Always Tomorrow*, in which it is associated
    with the frustrated romance between Clifford Groves,
    played by Fred MacMurray, and his former employee,
    Norma Miller (Barbara Stanwyck).

13. The symbolic significance of Estrella's name is also
    discussed by John Hopewell, *Out of the Past ...*, p. 211,
    and Peter Evans and Robin Fiddian, 'Victor Erice's *El
    Sur ...*', p. 129.

14. Peter Evans and Robin Fiddian, 'Victor Erice's *El Sur
    ...*', p. 129, observe that the 'separation of the family
    into nuclei living at opposite ends of a divided nation
    ... constitute a paradigm of Spain's domestic disinte-
    gration. ...'

Matador

Matador, Almodóvar's fifth full-length commercial film, received its première in Madrid on March 3, 1986, and has since been seen in many other countries. In relation to the film's origins, Almodóvar has explained that at first his intention was to make a film in which the two main characters were a film director and a dwarf actress whose closest friend was a murderer. The latter, because of severe personality problems, remained unaware of the crimes he had committed. Gradually, the murderer became the principal source of fascination and, since it was felt that for him killing was a kind of art, it became clear that he should also be a bullfighter. By the time that Almodóvar came to write the script, the story of the bullfighter was also interwoven with that of a female lawyer, and the narrative of the film as a whole had changed greatly from that originally envisaged.[1]

In all his previous films Almodóvar had been both director and script-writer. In *Matador*, however, he was assisted in the writing of the script by Jesús Ferrero, largely on account of increasing demands on his own time, and has generously acknowledged his debt and gratitude for the quality and style which Ferrero brought to certain aspects of the film's dialogue:

> Working with another writer was something I found very positive. Some of the dialogue is entirely his, probably the best-written passages in

> the film. . . There is one scene which is his and his
> alone, the scene in which she [María Cardenal]
> takes him [Diego Montes] to the secret museum
> where she keeps her mementos. . . .[2]

The dialogue of *Matador* is highly literary and well
crafted, although many of its colloquialisms and much
of its irreverent wit is pure Almodóvar.

As far as the film's themes are concerned, Almodóvar
has himself stated that his principal aim was to highlight the relationship between sexual pleasure and
death, and, in conjunction with those themes, to bring
together two lovers, male and female, who are obsessed with both.[3] These are, of course, themes which
are deeply ingrained in Spanish culture and history. As
far as Spanish film is concerned, the combination of sex
and death can be seen in many of the films studied
here, though not quite, perhaps, in the way in which
Almodóvar integrates them. Amongst foreign films he
has mentioned as influences *Cat People, Duel in the Sun*
and *Empire of the Senses. Duel in the Sun* is actually used
in the course of *Matador*, much as Erice uses sequences
from other films as points of reference in his own work.
But it is, perhaps, *Empire of the Senses*, with its potent
mixture of eroticism and death, which suggests itself as
an even more powerful influence. Indeed, Almodóvar
has himself suggested that Jesús Ferrero's contribution
to the script helped to make it into 'something more
Japanese.'[4]

Like so many of Buñuel's films, *Matador* has attracted
high praise and admiration from some and scorn and
condemnation from others. Writing in *Sight and Sound*,
for example, Verina Glaessner concludes that 'Almodóvar's directorial fluency and daring in *Matador* confirm
him as the most interesting and exciting film-maker

working in Spain today.'[5] In a more general article in the same journal, Lawrence O'Toole, suggests, in contrast, that 'Almodóvar is like a jokester who'll go to any extreme to get off a good crack, and he tends to turn shrill.'[6] Almodóvar himself is doubtless delighted to have stirred up such controversy.

Matador begins with a sequence in which an ex-bullfighter, Diego Montes, masturbates as he watches a 'snuff' movie. The word 'matador' appears over a shot of a woman being drowned in a bath, while the other credits accompany equally violent assaults on women: a decapitation; a woman punched in the face. The colours throughout the sequence — orange, blue and red — are themselves violent and garish, and the soundtrack consists of the protests, howls and screams of the victims, accompanied by discordant music. In a sense this opening is reminiscent of the famous initial sequence of Buñuel's *Un Chien andalou* — indeed, a close-up of a razor here accompanies the murder of a woman in the bath — and the effect is just as powerful. On the other hand, Buñuel's purpose was to shock the audience of his film into watching it more attentively; Almodóvar's to equate from the very outset sexual pleasure and death, the two central themes of the film.

The second sequence reveals the same man, Diego Montes, giving a class at his bullfighting school in Madrid on the art of killing the bull, in the course of which he emphasizes the need to kill the bull well. To fail to do so, he observes, is unfortunate both for the bullfighter and the bull, and to this he adds that, as soon as the bull appears in the ring, the bullfighter needs to watch it from a distance in order to see precisely how he will conduct the fight. At this point the observations on bullfighting become, in a quite extraordinary and marvellously stylish episode, a sexual encounter between a young man and a strikingly beautiful woman, María Cardenal, a Madrid lawyer who, later in the film, will become Diego Montes's lover. The events revealed to us now are not, however, occurring simultaneously with the lesson in bullfighting but have already happened in the past and are seen in a kind of 'vision' by the hypersensitive Angel, one of Diego's young pupils.[7] The parallels between the bullfight and the sexual encounter are precise. The camera reveals María Cardenal, first walking, then seated in a square, and a young man approaching from a distance across a sand-coloured surface strongly reminiscent of a bullring. As he does so, María watches him closely in order to determine how she will conduct her particular fight. Indeed, when she takes the young man to a room, the sequence becomes a series of closely orchestrated juxtapositions in which the couple's love-making alternates with shots of bullfighting moves in the ring at Diego's school. His reference to the spot between the bull's shoulders into which the sword must be driven is accompanied by María's kissing her lover on the nape of the neck at the top of the spine. A pass with the cloak has its parallel in María's sweeping off her gown. The thrust of the bull's horns finds its echo in the man's penetration of María. And finally, the sword-thrust, producing the bull's death, becomes, in a quite remarkable climax, María killing her lover in the full ecstacy of orgasm with a long pin which she drives through the back of his neck. The second sequence, emphasizing the parallel between intense sexual pleasure and death, is thus linked to the first, and, although Diego Montes and María Cardenal have not yet met, identifies them as kindred spirits whose destiny will become inextricably interwoven as the film unfolds. As to the sustained parallel between the bullfight and sexual activity, it goes without saying that the relationship between the two things is deeply embedded in the Hispanic consciousness from ancient times: the bull as the embodiment of male sexual power and prowess; the sexual symbolism of the horns and the thrust; the way in which the bullfighter gracefully manoeuvres the bull in a kind of extended foreplay; and, of course, the final climactic thrust of the sword, together with the sense of release that equates the death of the bull with orgasm.[8]

Given the above, it is no accident that Diego Montes, having been prevented from fighting bulls by an accident in the ring, should turn his attention to women. Indeed, throughout the film allusions to bullfighting and sex are virtually indistinguishable. When, later in the film, Diego takes María Cardenal to his bullfighting museum, her observation, 'I like a good performance,' refers as much to her sexual relationship with him as to any bullfight she may have seen. In the early part of the film, moreover, Diego is for his pupil, Angel, a role model in more ways than one, and their initial conversation about bullfighting soon turns, significantly, to the topic of women. Angel's revelation that he has not yet experienced sexual relations with a woman draws from Diego the suggestion, angrily refuted by the young man, that he is not only abnormal but also homosexual, and this in turn drives Angel to assert that he will prove his masculinity once and for all.[9] The theme of male sexuality is thus associated not only with bullfighting but also with 'machismo', and in that context another powerful and age-old Hispanic topic is worked into the story. For all the modernity of *Matador* in terms of its sexual explicitness and cinematic style, its themes are largely traditional, and the links with Buñuel are frequently very close.

In this particular context the reasons for Angel's

sexually arrested development have clear Buñuelian echoes and, at a fairly early stage in the film, introduce another of its central themes: religion. In his opening conversation with Diego, Angel reveals that his family — in reality, his mother — is a member of the Catholic organization, Opus Dei, and that he spends his time not so much pursuing girls but 'praying and keeping fit.'[10] Angel's mother, Berta, is introduced, revealingly, by her harsh imperious voice, reminiscent of Bernarda Alba, the most famous oppressor in Spanish literature, demanding to know what he is doing behind the locked door of his bedroom. In a subsequent scene at the dinner table, the nature of the mother-son relationship is even more tellingly revealed, as, indeed, is that with her deceased husband. Regarding the latter as quite mad, she considers Angel to be a 'chip off the old block' and allows him to live at home only on certain conditions, the most important of which are that he attend church regularly and allow himself to be guided by his 'spiritual advisor.' Little wonder, then, that the boy should prove to be weak, passive, totally mother-dominated, and, in consequence of the stifling moral and religious nature of his home life, overwhelmed by feelings of guilt and inadequacy. The centrality of religion to Angel's life, if only as an inescapable presence, is vividly revealed in the following sequence in church when, as he makes his exit, the camera reveals three images of the crucified Christ. In setting Angel alongside them, Almodóvar points not to his redemption but to his anguish and suffering.

Responding to Diego's suggestions of sexual inadequacy, Angel is driven initially to voyeurism, the easiest way of releasing sexual frustration. A close-up of a young woman drying herself after taking a shower and seen through a circular lens is revealed to be the object viewed by Angel through his binoculars. The extent of his excitement is also powerfully suggested here by a flash of lightning and crashing thunder, a device used by Almodóvar throughout the film to accompany and underline the feelings of the characters. Certainly, Angel is suddenly seized by sexual desire and swept along by a storm of uncontrollable feeling as he leaves the house and follows the girl, Eva, who is Diego's girlfriend, along the street. Overtaking her, he seizes her, pushes her over the bonnet of her car, holds a knife to her throat and attempts to rape her. In part, of course, Eva is the object of Angel's sexual attentions precisely because she is Diego's girlfriend, and to emulate his teacher and role model Angel must possess her too. On the other hand, the confused Angel, tossed around by his emotions like a leaf in the wind, is no Diego, and his efforts to prove himself on Eva achieve the precise opposite, all portrayed by Almodóvar in a characteristic balancing act of melodrama, pathos and outrageous comedy. The rape ends, for example, with his apologies and with Eva slapping his face: the roles of aggressor and victim reversed. Moreover, when in the process of hurrying away Eva falls and cuts her cheek, Angel faints at the sight of blood. On a psychological level, as far as he is concerned, the episode is, of course, a disaster, for, thwarted by guilt and conscience, his attempts to be a man merely prove to him that he is not and produce an even deeper sense of humiliation, heightened by Eva's modern-day coolness in the face of Angel's desperate groping. And when later, in an interview with the police and in the young man's presence, Eva not only refuses to bring charges but informs the police inspector that Angel ejaculated prematurely — 'He came between my legs' — his last vestige of self-esteem is cruelly and comically stripped away.

The contrast between Angel and Eva, the old and the new Spain, is evident too in their parents, or rather their mothers. Unlike the narrow-minded, bigotted, morally intransigent Berta, Eva's mother, Pilar, is a delightful embodiment of an altogether more superficial approach to life which rejects not only the image which the traditional family projects but embraces the glamour associated with her daughter's budding career as a model. She is less concerned with the fact that Eva has been raped than with the possibility of the neighbours finding out. We can only imagine how Berta would have reacted. At the police station she is less interested in the facts of the case and the presence of the culprit than in her daughter being late for a casting session. In her dress too Pilar has been greatly influenced by her daughter and delights in the evident freedom of the new Spain. In portraying her with a lovely sense of irony, Almodóvar suggests not a middle-aged woman on the edge of a nervous breakdown but someone who, having tasted freedom, is determined to enjoy it to the full.[11]

Angel's presence at the police station is explained by the fact that, if previously he felt an overwhelming sense of guilt, his attempted violation of Eva increases it ten-fold, to the point where he feels the need to make a public confession — to the police, not to a priest — of his badness. Indeed, having seen at the police station photographs of the victims of four murders which the police are currently investigating (the two men have in fact been murdered by María Cardenal, the two women by Diego Montes), Angel seizes the opportunity to assuage his guilt further by admitting to the crimes. Once more there is something very Buñuelian here, in particular in the portrayal of someone driven to such lengths by guilt that his predicament becomes, in its very seriousness, comic. The spectacle of Angel behind bars when even his attempted rape of Eva failed is poignantly ironic. And there is further irony in the fact that the lawyer who defends him is herself responsible for two of the murders: María Cardenal.

María's introduction into Angel's affairs soon brings her, through him, into contact with the other murderer, Diego. The innocent and wrongly jailed Angel is thus the unwitting catalyst of the love affair which unites the two murderers and sets in motion the events which lead to its momentous climax. As far as María and Diego are concerned, they are presented by Almodóvar, from the moment of their first meeting, as 'star-cross'd' lovers bound by a common destiny. Seeing María leave Angel's house, Diego follows her to a cinema and goes inside as the climax of the Hollywood film, *Duel in the Sun*, is seen on the screen. As in the case of Agustín, who in *The South* watches in the cinema an episode from a film which reflects his own experience, so here the ending of *Duel in the Sun* points to the relationship and the fate of María and Diego. In the film the heroine (played by Jennifer Jones), concealed behind rocks, shoots the man she loves (Gregory Peck) higher up on a cliff and is in turn shot. They crawl towards each other and embrace in the moment of death, she saying to him, 'I had to do it, I had to do it', he to her, 'Yes, I understand.' As they watch the on-screen events, María and Diego are physically distanced from each other but contained in the same shot and are both totally absorbed by the events they are watching. The title of the film, in its suggestion of a pair engaged in conflict — 'duel' — and its allusion to a star — 'sun' — will become more and more relevant to them.

The notion of a couple, of a man and a woman who are destined for each other, is suggested in a variety of

ways. When, for example, María Cardenal makes her
very first appearance in the film, she is dressed in a
black and white check jacket and skirt. Later, when
Diego Montes is watching a video tape of a bullfight, he
sees Maria amongst the spectators, on this occasion
dressed in a black and white blouse. At this moment
Diego's sweater is seen to consist of a dark blue, almost
black colour, with a regular white pattern, while earlier, when he follows her to the cinema, he is wearing a
jacket whose black and white colouring is a variation
on her check suit. The parallel is established too in
terms of the costume worn by the bullfighter. Attending a fashion show, María wears an extraordinarily
striking outfit distinguished by its flowing red and
yellow cloak.[12] At Diego's bullfighting school she wraps
herself in his bullfighter's cloak while on the video
screen she watches Diego wearing the same cloak during his career in the bullring. In addition, María's
appearance — in particular her facial appearance —
evokes that of the bullfighter: her black hair drawn
tight to her head, her face pale, her eyebrows and
lashes theatrically highlighted.

Their love affair is, from its very beginning, conducted in terms of the bullfight itself, combining its
essential elements of skill, style, passion, danger and
death. It is no coincidence, therefore, that their first
sexual encounter should occur at Diego's bullfighting
school or that incidents and allusions should mirror the
bullfight. In the first place the black and white of
María's suit brings to mind the sharp contrasts of light
and shade, of sun and shadow, so characteristic of the
bullring. María's assumption of the bullfigher's cloak,
casting her in the role of the 'torero' and Diego in the
role of the bull, precedes her attempt to kill him with
her long pin. Thwarting her and seizing the pin, Di-

ego's observation — 'I think I deserve it' — is reminiscent of the bullfighter's reward for a good performance,
usually the bull's ear. And her failure to kill him draws
from Diego some advice based on his own experience
in the ring: 'At the moment of killing, do not hesi-
tate... It is one of the golden rules of bullfighting'.
When, in a later episode, Diego is seen watching video
films of bullfights, he is clearly a changed man, as
absorbed now by the challenge and excitement of María's
arrival in his life as by any of his experiences in the
ring.

The ritual of the bullfight is also distinguished from
ancient times by a sense of inevitability, of death at the
end of a contest which, however skillful, thrilling and
passionate, can have only one conclusion. In this respect the notion, described earlier, of María and Diego
as a pair meant for each other, is increasingly interwoven with the theme of inevitable fate, astral influence
and death. After their first encounter, for example,
María seeks to avoid Diego, aware of the danger he
represents, but he tracks her down to her office, drawn
to her inescapably: 'María, we are condemned to be
together. We cannot escape it.' In a later episode in the
house where María displays momentos of Diego's days
in the bullring, their dialogue suggests that in him
there is a part of her, in her a part of him, and thus a
mutual and inescapable attraction: 'in every male criminal there is something that is female.' 'In every murderess
there is something masculine.' And when, later, Diego
observes María through the window of a store, a voice-
over (in reality the voice of Julia, the police psychiatrist)
is used by Almodóvar to relate a definition of an eclipse
to the lovers themselves: 'When two astral bodies meet,
their light appears to be extinguished, but ... they
acquire a new dark and blazing brightness. . . .' In this

context too the black and white associated with María and Diego can be seen to suggest pairs that are not merely similar but also interlocking, like light and dark, sun and moon. It is in terms of this inevitable cosmic background that the film's conclusion is expressed.[13]

Angel, meanwhile, continues to claim responsibility for the murders committed by María and Diego and is driven into an increasingly neurotic state in which he is assaulted by constant visions. They include the two murders committed by Diego, one girl strangled during sexual intercourse, another drowned in her bath. But even though he now knows the identity of the murderers, he continues to claim responsibility for them. In one sense, as has been seen already, a crippling feeling of guilt leads to a need for self-abasement and punishment. On the other hand, just as his violation of Eva stemmed from a deep-seated need to emulate his 'teacher', Diego, so his claim to be the murderer is rooted in the same desire. In this respect, of course, his visions prove to be invaluable, allowing him to confess to details of the crimes which only the murderer could possibly know. In a film in which María and Diego are a fascinating and mysterious duo, Angel is also an arresting study of someone torn between the conflicting demands of religion and sex and destroyed in the process.

The last part of *Matador* is dominated by the final encounter of María and Diego and by the theme of the eclipse. As Eva and her mother, Pilar, watch television, the announcer's voice refers to the eclipse which is soon to take place and which has attracted hundreds of scientists. The announcer describes the nature and effect of an eclipse in some detail: 'the moon will conceal the sun. The sky will grow dark. . . The birds will fly to their nests. The animals will enter their dens, believing that night has fallen, not realizing that in a few minutes the sun will appear again. In consequence the lives of these poor unthinking creatures, slaves of their instincts, are thrown into complete confusion. . . .' The allusion to the instinctive behaviour of animals is immediately set in a broader context, including the human, by Pilar — 'The whole world is like that.' — and is effectively illustrated by Eva, now rejected by Diego but unable to forget her feelings for him. Indeed, the notion of human beings manipulated by their emotions, be it love, self-disgust or guilt, is evident in all the major characters of the film. On the one hand, Eva's message for Diego is witness to her unchanging passion for him — 'Dear Diego. I love you. Eva.' — while, on the other, he is obsessed with María: 'I am mad.' In this regard the characters of *Matador* are as much driven men and women as those of Lorca's *Blood Wedding* in which the notion of fate is also a key element and in which planetary influence, in the form of the moon, also plays a significant part. To this extent, for all its modern trappings, Almodóvar's film is again seen to exhibit fundamental Spanish themes.[14]

The ending of *Matador* is, like much of what has preceded it, highly ritualistic. Diego and María arrive at her house outside Madrid where they have planned their final hours of pleasure. The theme of pleasure and ecstacy, leading to death, is unfolded here in a sequence which is beautifully stylized, exquisitely shot and extremely operatic. Diego, dressed in his bullfighter's costume, spreads his cloak on the floor with a sweeping gesture. María, dressed in the pseudo-bullfighter's cloak referred to earlier, scatters roses over the cloak that will be their bed. Seen from above, the setting has all the appearance of the bullring in which the contest is about to begin. The initial stages, equivalent to the bullfighter's testing out of the bull, are pure foreplay as Diego strokes the length of María's body with the petals of a rose. The eroticism of the scene is greatly enhanced, moreover, by the sheer beauty and interplay of its colours, always one of the most striking aspects of an Almodóvar film. Pinks, golds, reds, the reflection of firelight, all create a wonderfully languorous effect, which is further accentuated by the slow caressing movements of the lovers and the lyrical song on the soundtrack: 'Wait for me in heaven, my love, if you leave before me. Wait for me, for soon I'll be where you have gone already. . . .' The song, of course, acts as a kind of chorus in which the conclusion of the love scene is anticipated, as well as a voice expressing the lovers' feelings. As the scene unfolds, pleasure is also increasingly related to death. So María asks of Diego: 'Would you like to see me dead?' He replies: 'Yes, and I'd like you to see me dead.' The climax of the sequence, in all senses of the word, arrives with the eclipse. As the moon passes across the sun, obliterating it, so Diego and María achieve mutual orgasm, she kills him with the pin and then shoots herself. To that extent the moment of total ecstasy is, for them, frozen in the moment of death, and thus never lost. As Angel, Eva, the police inspector and Julia arrive at the house only to see the bodies of the dead lovers, Angel observes that he could not prevent their death, and the police inspector adds that he has never seen anyone so happy. The themes of fate, death and pleasure are thus effectively entwined.

Whatever the controversy that has raged around *Matador*, both inside and outside Spain, it cannot be denied that, as is the case with many of Dalí's paintings, the film makes an unforgettable impression and many of its startling sequences and images remain in the mind long afterwards. In many ways it is, of course, a deeply Spanish film, for its fundamental preoccupations with passion, death and religion are themes which are central to the Spanish cultural tradition. That said, Almodóvar's treatment of those themes is distinctly modern and could never have been contemplated during the dictatorship. The freedom with which sex, in particular, is portrayed in *Matador* is highly characteristic of post-Franco Spain, which is one reason at least why Almodóvar has struck a chord with Spanish audiences.

Notes

1. See Almodóvar's account of the film's origins in Nuria Vidal, *El cine de Pedro Almodóvar*, Barcelona: Destinolibro, 1990, pp. 159–161.

2. Nuria Vidal, *El cine de Pedro Almodóvar* . . ., p. 161.

3. Nuria Vidal, *El cine de Pedro Almodóvar* . . ., p. 170.

4. Nuria Vidal, *El cine de Pedro Almodóvar* . . ., p. 159.

5. *Sight and Sound*, September 1992, p. 48.

6. In 'Almodóvar in Bondage', *Sight and Sound*, Autumn 1990, pp. 270–273.

7. Although the sequence is a 'vision', it is presented as if it were actually happening, and there is no attempt on Almodóvar's part to distinguish it in terms of its reality from the events which precede and follow it. Almodóvar makes this precise point and compares his technique in this respect with that of Buñuel in Nuria Vidal, *El cine*

as they are, there is no element of deceit. In this respect I am a disciple of Buñuel. When Buñuel films a dream, he does so using the same kind of light, of setting, and gives the same impression of reality as in the rest of the film. . . .'

8. Lawrence O'Toole, *Sight and Sound*. . ., p. 272, suggests: 'The murder scenarios in *What Have I Done to Deserve Tis?*, *Matado* and *Law of Desire*, which show the director's outlandish methods of dispatch . . . are simply a means to an end — the end of the movie. They're just not satisfying on a basic narrative level. . . .' A comment of this kind seems completely inappropriate to this most striking and stylish sequene in *Matador*.

9. As the only gay director amongst the four studied here, it is inevitable that in Almodóvar's hands the theme of 'machismo' should be treated somewhat ironically.

10. The line could quite easily come from a Buñuel film. The sense of moral and religious oppression and the guilt which it instils in Angel invite comparison with Buñuel's *Viridiana*, both in relation to Don Jaime and to Viridiana herself.

11. Almodóvar makes the point that the two mothers 'co-exist in this country and in a sense represent the two faces of Spain'. See Nuria Vidal, *El cine d Pedro Almodóvar*. . ., p. 177.

12. In relation to María andDiego, Almodóvar has, in fact, pointed out, as this study has suggested, that 'their roles are interchangeable according to the circumstances. There are moments when she is the bullfighter and vice-versa.' See Nuria Vidal, *El cine de edro Almodóvar*. . ., p. 166.

13. In the interviw on *Matador* in Nuria Vidal's book, Almodóvar notes that he is not particularly interested in stars but seems to refer to them constantly in his work: 'When I write the script, I try to be as pure and as

work: 'When I write the script, I try to be as pure and as irrational as possible, and things emerge which have nothing to do with my daily life.' See p. 162.

14. It is, perhaps, worth mentioning that, like Lorca, Almodóvar is from the south of Spain and doubtless shares much of his predecessor's background in relation to the notions about fate and death so ingrained in the culture of that part of the country.

Women on the Verge of a Nervous Breakdown

Women on the Verge of a Nervous Breakdown, premièred in Madrid on March 23, 198 is Almodóvar's best known and, in commercial terms, most successful film. It has also received widespread critical acclaim. In 1988, for example, it was named best foreign film by both the New York Film Critics' Circle and the American National Board of Review of Motion Pictures, and in 1989 gained an Oscar nomination in the same category. Within Spain itself it received numerous accolades: the Goya award in 1989; the best picture award from the Asociación de Escritores Cinemato-gráficos de Andalucía in the same year; and it was also chosen as best film by Spanish television critics and viewers. In addition, Carmen Maura has won many awards for her performance as Pepa, including the Goya, while Almodóvar himself received a Goya for best director.[1] Here there appear once more many of the actors from Almodóvar's previous films — Carmen Maura herself, Antonio Banderas, Julieta Serrano, Chus Lampreave — creating a team spirit which contributes greatly to the overall brilliance of the acting. On the other hand, *Women on the Verge. . .* was also to create a much publicized rupture between Almodóvar and Carmen Maura, infuriated by his treatment of her at the Oscar ceremony. She has not appeared in a subsequent film of his.

As far as its origins are concerned, *Women on the Verge...* began as an idea which Almodóvar had long had for a film based on a monologue spoken by a woman alone and in a single setting, similar in that respect to Cocteau's *La Voix humaine*. Subsequently, other possibilities suggested themselves, in particular the events of the previous forty-eight hours which had contributed and led to the woman's present predicament. Later still, in the process of writing, the notion of the single woman abandoned in her room became more complex, introducing other women and the world outside, and the telephone, central to the original idea, and on which the woman awaits a call from her lover, was replaced by an answerphone, which does not require her to stay at home and on which her lover's voice can actually be heard.[2]

In *Women on the Verge...* the influence of Almodóvar's other films is also, of course, important. He has himself suggested that the character of Pepa derives from that of Tina in *Law of Desire*, but there are also links with Pepi in *Pepi, Luci, Bom...* Bom in this film has also in a sense become Candela in *Women on the Verge...* and there are other anticipations of her in the character of Riza Niro in *Labyrinth of Passion*. Paulina, the female lawyer, recalls, despite her differences, María Cardenal in *Matador*, while Carlos and Lucía have their parallels in Angel and Berta, the son and mother in the same film.[3] It would, of course, be surprising if a director's earlier work did not feed into subsequent projects, but Almodóvar has also drawn attention to other, foreign influences, in particular the American director, Billy Wilder, observing not only that *Women on the Verge...* is his most Wilder-like film but that there is a marked similarity between Carmen Maura's Pepa and Shirley MacLaine's role in *The Apartment*.[4] Even so, the fact its most serious moments, there is an irreverent and subversive humour in *Women on the Verge...* that is entrely Almodóvar's and that distinguishes him from any other director.

The titles appear against a collage of shots of elegant women. 'A Film by Pedro Almodóvar', for example, is set against a background divided into three sections: top left, the lower half of a woman's smiling face; bottom centre, a woman's right eye; top right a woman's left eye. The title of the film itself appears over the left-hand side of a woman's face, while later on an arrangement of women's eyes is accompanied by scissors, thereby underlining the idea of collage and cut-outs. In a sense the notion of women cut up, dissected and anatomized brings to mind the opening sequene of *Matador* in which women are literally chopped into pieces, but the comparison is one which merely serves to highlight the difference between the two films. The cut-outs here are stylish, elegant, witty, suggestive of an altogether lighter tone in the context of which the potentially serious implications of the film's title dissolve into something rather more ironic. In addition, the elegance and artificiality of this opening serves as an introduction to the world of television and film in which the main character, Pepa and her lover, Iván, work. Looked at in another way, the cut-outs suggest the idea of fragmentation; bits and pieces. In this respect they point to lives confused and disrupted, one of the film's main themes, but in a formal sense they also suggest the separate and sometimes bewildering incidents of the opening twenty minutes, the individual bits of the puzzle or the jigsaw that eventually begin to come together in a meaningful and satisfying way.[5] Finally, the song which accompanies the titles — 'Oh, Unhappy Woman' — has a somewhat sentimental, romantic quality, the kind of seriousness evoked by the film's title, which, in the context of the film itself, becomes ironic, promising one thing but delivering another, and revealing in the process Almodóvar's love of walking a tightrope composed of opposites.

The film itself begins with a sequence in which Pepa, asleep, dreams of Iván. He is seen holding a microphone as he casually strolls past a number of women of different professions and from different countries, addressing them as he does so: 'My life is meaningless without you. Will you marry me. . . I can't live without you. I love you, want you, need you. . . You are the geisha in my life. . . I'm all yours. I accept you as you are, darling.' The words are, of course, from a script, for Iván does voice-overs and dubbing for films, and there is a striking difference between the potentially serious meaning of the words and their emptiness in the context in which they are spoken.[6] In this sequence Iván is, literally, a strolling actor playing a part and saying things he does not mean. But Pepa's dream, of course, immediately relates the notion of Iván as actor to her own relationship with him. In that too he has uttered words that had no real meaning, drawn in all probability from who knows how many well-thumbed scripts. The link between role-play and reality, fiction and life, is thus established very early in the film.

This theme is then developed in two separate sequences involving, first, Iván, and then Pepa. In the first of these Iván is seen in the studio in the process of dubbing a western, *Johnny Guitar*, starring Joan Crawford and Sterling Hayden. In this sequence the male character accuses the woman of betraying him: 'How many men have you had to forget?' The woman's replies are not heard here but are filled in, in the second sequence, by Pepa, who proceeds to deny the male character's accusations:

> He: How many men have you had to forget?
> She: As many as the women you can remember.
> He: Don't go.
> She: I haven't moved.
> He: Say something nice.
> She: What do you want me to say?
> He: Lie. 'You've been waiting for me'. Say it.
> She: I waited for you all these years.
> He: Say you'd have died without me.
> She: I'd have died without you.
> He: Say you love me as I love you.
> She: I love you as you love me.
> He: Thank you, thank you very much.

In the scene as a whole the real-life relationship of Pepa and Iván is, of course, ironically reversed, for it is he, the betrayer, who plays the man betrayed, and she, the deceived woman, who plays the deceiver. The reversal of roles, especially in Iván's case, draws attention to his facility as an actor, for he plays the innocent with complete conviction. As far as Pepa is concerned, the words she speaks in the role, which requires her to lie — 'I'd have died without you.' — are absolutely true in relation to her feelings for Iván. Almodóvar offers us here, then, a sequence from his own film in which the characters Pepa and Iván are themselves playing parts in another film which are the opposite of what they, the characters, are in reality. Indeed, no sooner does he finish 'acting' than Iván reverts to his true colours by leaving a message on Pepa's answerphone to the effect that he is leaving her, but even in this real-life situation his lines smack of pretence and of a performance that is not genuine, his real motives concealed beneath a glib façade:

> Pepa . . . Put all my stuff in a suitcase. I'm leaving on a trip tomorrow. I'll pick it up and say goodbye . . . I don't deserve all your kindness. . . .

The interplay of fiction and reality thus constitutes a key idea in the film, as is the case, indeed, in *Matador* and many of the other films studied here. In *Women on the Verge. . .*, moreover, it is not merely a case of 'the games that lovers play', for the women in question, increasingly caught up in the complexities of their love lives, become not only puppet-like characters manipulated by events in an action that is ever more frantic and frenetic, but, in the sense that the film itself draws on the long tradition of comedy and farce, actors in their own story.

From the very outset the theme of love, serious in itself, is placed in the context of farce, much of the early part of the film focused on the growing chaos in Pepa's life. It begins, for instance, with her sleeping late, discovering Iván is leaving her, finding out she is pregnant by him and phoning the woman she mistakenly thinks he is going off with. These separate but related episodes then lead into a more sustained sequence in Pepa's flat during which she hurls Iván's clothes into a suitcase, absentmindedly throws a lighted match onto the bed, setting it on fire, and douses the fire with a garden-hose, soaking the bedroom in the process. The ingredients of farce are many and complex, but incongruity, misunderstanding and the notion of people under pressure are undoubtedly amongst them and are handled by Almodóvar with total aplomb. There is, for instance, considerable incongruity in the fact that Pepa, the modern, independent, sophisticated, cool career woman, is placed at the centre of increasing chaos in her personal life. Subjected to that pressure, moreover, she reacts in a sometimes instinctive and spontaneous way — the throwing of the lighted match — which merely increases it by creating further complications, a kind of chain reaction. And this in turn leads to the spectacle of an otherwise rational and dignified human being behaving in ways which are both irrational and undignified, a key element in farce in general. As far as misunderstanding is concerned, Pepa's assumption that the woman she telephones — in effect Lucía, Iván's lover of twenty years ago — is the woman he plans to go away with, is a simple error which has enormous consequences, bringing into the story a woman with a history of mental imbalance who later in the film sets out to shoot Iván.

The ingredients mentioned above, crucial as they are, are nevertheless the bare bones around which other important elements are woven. From the outset, for instance, much humour is derived not merely from the fact that Pepa believes Lucía to be the other woman in Iván's life, but also from the way in which Lucía is presented. She is first seen as a woman who, although she is probably around fifty, constantly attempts to appear young, painting her face, donning wigs, dressing in brightly coloured clothes: 'Time stands still when I wear those clothes.' The spectacle is, of course, bizarre, and no more so than when, a little later, she unwittingly passes Pepa on the stairs to Iván's flat, arrayed in a kind of leopard-skin dress with matching hat which might well suit a younger and more glamorous woman but which on Lucía looks more like a lampshade. Again, when Pepa leaves a note for Iván and Lucía attempts to read it, she is obliged, because of her age, to hold the note at arm's length in order to focus on it properly. The serious business of love and rivalry is thus rendered absurd by the context in which it is placed and by Almodóvar's wonderful sense of the ridiculous. It becomes even more hilarious, of course, when it is subsequently revealed that Lucía has only recently been released from a mental institution: in short, the woman Pepa believes to be her rival for Iván's love is totally deranged.

Two other sequences may be singled out to illustrate Almodóvar's delightful and subversive humour. The first concerns the taxi in which Pepa pursues Lucía, urging the taxi driver to 'follow that taxi.' Using as his starting point a cliché from Hollywood films, Almodóvar proceeds to send it up in every conceivable way. The taxi driver himself, with his yellow hat and bright green shirt, is the total opposite of his macho American counterpart, while the taxi itself, furnished with leopard-skin seat covers and offering to customers all manner of amenities, from magazines to mambo music, is more department store than vehicle. In short, the traditional melodramatic car chase of American films is transformed into a farce in which the pursuers are an eccentric taxi driver and a passenger distraught by love, and the pursued a mentally unbalanced older woman. The second sequence also involves subversion: on this occasion, of advertisements on television. At home Pepa watches an advert in which she plays the part of a mother who uses 'Omo' to wash her clothes. She reveals herself to be the mother of the notorious 'Crossroads Killer' who, after a murder, invariably comes home with a terribly blood-stained shirt. As she places the shirt in the washing machine, the police arrive in hot pursuit of the killer and seeking the incriminating shirt. When the mother produces the shirt, it is, of course, whiter than white, and the police depart completely frustrated. In this sequence Almodóvar has simply taken the stock situation of washing-powder adverts — children dirtying and staining clothes — and replaced it with something which fits the situation perfectly but is quite unexpected. Moreover, he caps the whole thing with a totally outrageous joke as the mother triumphantly addresses us: 'Ecce Omo.' This and the taxi sequence illustrate Almodóvar's love of placing within the narrative of his films individual comic episodes which are in themselves absolute gems, jewels in an already glittering piece.[7]

The events described so far, focusing for the most part on the growing disruption of Pepa's life, constitute the first third of the film. The remaining two thirds involve much greater complications and can be divided structurally into three broad sections: two extended sequences located in Pepa's flat, and a final car chase. The first of the two sequences introduces into Pepa's already complicated life three other characters: a young woman friend, Candela; and a young man, Carlos and his girl-friend Marisa. In the early part of the sequence much of the humour derives from the fact that a familiar situation is given an unexpected twist. There is nothing unusual or comic, for example, in two young people arriving to view a flat. What makes their arrival comic is the fact that Carlos is Iván's son and is therefore astonished to see his father's photograph on another woman's bedside table. Moreover, the introductions, which, in another situation, would be uninteresting become, in this context, quite hilarious:

> Carlos: This is Marisa.
> Pepa: Nice to meet you.
> Marisa: I'm his fiancée.

> Pepa: I'm his father's lover.

As well as this, the traditional conducted tour in the course of which the prospective buyer is informed of the attractive features of the house is wickedly subverted here when Pepa explains away the charred bed:

> Excuse the mess. Life has been hectic lately.[8]

And finally, another witty touch is introduced when Carlos proceeds to repair the telephone so that Pepa can receive incoming calls from his father.

The pace of the sequence, so far controlled and restrained and marked by a good deal of verbal humour, erupts into sudden frenetic movement when Candela attempts to throw herself from the terrace wall to the street below and the others rush to haul her to safety. The quiet and delicate ironies of the early part of the sequence become in a flash the desperation and the indignities of farce: Candela's anguished cries as she hangs by her fingertips; the urgent advice of her friends as they try to stop her falling; the indignity of her predicament as, skirt up over her bottom, she is hauled to safety. The secret of farce is, of course, that it must be played seriously, as is the case here, the movements, gestures, faces and voices of the actors expressing the fear, panic and relief of the situation. Almodóvar understands all this perfectly well, and he knows too how to cap a scene with a wonderfully appropriate, seriously intentioned but beautifully comic line. As everyone collapses, and a sense of relief takes over, Pepa instructs Carlos: 'Fetch my tranquilizers from the kitchen.'

Candela's explanation of her suicide attempt again places love in the context of farce, and to that extent interweaves her experience with that of Pepa. Having lost her heart to a handsome young man some three months previously, she has since discovered that he and his friends are Shi'ite terrorists and suspects that, having harboured them in her flat, she will be accused of involvement in their plot to hijack a plane. Genuinely moving on the one hand, Candela's feelings of sorrow and desperation become absurd precisely because the ordinariness of an unexceptional young woman's love is placed against the background of dangerous, international events. In the sense that she, like Pepa, is used and abused by a man, Almodóvar has been accused of misogyny. The truth of the matter is surely that, if the women in *Women on the Verge. . .* are victims of men, they are also presented as warm, attractive, feeling, sympathetic individuals, infinitely superior to the cold and calculating men who take advantage of them. In making the situation comic, Almodóvar approaches them not only as women but as human beings, exploiting weaknesses and vulnerabilities that are as true of men as of women. As far as the plot is concerned, Candela's predicament introduces a further complication, for if she is accused of complicity in terrorism, she will need a defence lawyer. Having sought out Paulina Morales to this end, Pepa quickly discovers that she is in fact the other woman with whom Iván is planning a vacation.

The two extended sequences in the flat are separated by Pepa's attempts to get rid of Iván's suitcase and his efforts to recover it — events which at one point are quite brilliantly orchestrated by Almodóvar into what is virtually the language of silent film. Just prior to this, though, he introduces one of those poignant cameos mentioned earlier, this time in the form of the female hall porter in Pepa's apartment block. Urged by Iván to lie to Pepa on his behalf, the woman (exquisitely played by Chus Lampreave) reveals herself to be a Jehovah's Witness to whom lies are anathema. The delicious humour of the situation lies in the fact that the plans of the cunning, calculating Iván are completely frustrated by a hall porter who is, incongruously, the complete opposite of the gossiping, untrustworthy types that such people are reputed to be. It is a comic note which sets the tone for the farcical sequence which now ensues.

It begins with Pepa emerging from the apartment block carrying the suitcase. As she does so, Iván is in a telephone kiosk nearby, attempting to contact Pepa about the suitcase. She walks past the kiosk, neither of them seeing the other. At the same time, a short distance away, Paulina Morales sits in her car, waiting for Iván to finish the call. As Pepa approaches and throws the suitcase into a skip, Paulina flattens herself on the seat of the car. Pepa, her objective accomplished, returns the way she came, once more passing the telephone kiosk. No sooner has she done so than Iván sees Lucía approaching along the street. Unable to escape, he slides to the floor in a crouching position as Lucía walks past. The humour here lies, firstly, in the fact that, of the four people whose lives are so entangled, three pursue their particular objectives within yards of each other yet in ignorance of each other's presence. Secondly, in the actions of Paulina and Iván, seeking to avoid being seen by Pepa and Lucía respectively, there is that familiar desperation which, in the absence of other forms of escape, leads to absurd and undignified physical postures. And thirdly, apart from the voice of Iván on the telephone, the whole of the sequence is silent, which has the effect of placing greater emphasis on the expressions and movements of the characters and therefore, in the context of the scene, of rendering them even more hilarious. In effect, Almodóvar has drawn here on the tradition of silent film and in so doing created a classic situation which is yet another demonstration of his comic gifts.[9]

The second extended sequence begins in the flat with the arrival of the police and Lucía, whom the policemen have encountered in the lift. In the early part of the episode one strand of the humour consists of Carlos's and Pepa's frantic attempts to account for Candela's agitation, attributed by them to her disappointment over a dress. A second strand lies in the policemen's frustration when their attempts to question Pepa about the Shi'ite terrorists are constantly thwarted by Lucía's insistence on asking her about Iván. What *Women on the Verge...* demonstrates above all is Almodóvar's capacity for unflagging and varied comic invention, for seeing in situations comic possibilities which are often quite unpredictable. Here, for instance, there is a fine irony in the fact that, although Pepa tells the police the truth about Iván and the identity of Carlos and Lucía, they find her story hard to believe; an irony which relates, of course, not only to her story here but to the story of the film as a whole. But the central section of the episode, stemming from the 'spiked' gazpacho, resorts to incongruity for its comic effect. In itself the police interrogation of Pepa and the others is, of course, serious, and is developed as such. Suspecting that someone in the flat knows more about the Shi'ite hijack plan than is being revealed, one of the police officers begins to increase the pressure, pressing Pepa and her friends for a truthful answer. In the sense that we, the audience, know that the gazpacho has been 'spiked', and the policemen do not, our anticipation of its inevitable effect does not for a moment lessen our delight when, at a point of high dramatic tension, in mid-sentence, the police officer suddenly yawns, sits down, and falls fast asleep. His example is then followed by others, including his colleague and the telephone engineer, until the flat is virtually littered with prone bodies. It is, of course, a spectacle of authority completely undermined and made to look ridiculous. To conclude the sequence, moreover, Almodóvar injects a sudden note of melodrama when Lucía seizes the police officer's gun, informs Pepa that she is mad, throws the gazpacho in her face, and makes her escape, evidently with the intention of shooting Iván. Taken as a whole, this extended sequence, beautifully put together, reveals very clearly Almodóvar's ability to interweave such disparate elements as irony, farce and melodrama.[10]

The stepped-up pace of the end of the sequence leads directly into the final chase, so characteristic of Hollywood films and here skillfully subverted by Almodóvar in every conceivable way. In the first place, in a moment of wonderful incongruity, the elegantly dressed Lucía hijacks a leather-suited motorcyclist, forcing him at gun-point to take her to the airport. Secondly, when Pepa flags down a taxi — more a case of 'Follow that bike' than 'Follow that car' — the taxi driver proves to be the eccentric we have seen before. There are some hilarious touches here, both of situation and of dialogue. When, for example, Pepa wipes her eyes in an attempt to clear them of the effect of the gazpacho, the taxi driver provides her with eye-drops, which he has added to his repetoire of merchandise. At one point his girl friend informs Pepa that she intends to buy a motorbike: 'With a bike who needs a man?' It is a beautifully droll comment on the heavily underlined sexual symbolism of motorcycles so commonly seen in advertising. But Pepa's reply is even better: 'Motor maintenance is easier than psychology. You can really get to know a bike.' The theme of the frentic car chase is thus filled with endearing touches, the traditional panic and screeching excitement rendered ludicrous. At the airport itself Lucía is on the point of shooting Iván when Pepa arrives, directs a luggage trolley at her and diverts the shot into the air. Saved by the woman he had abandoned, Iván suggests they should talk, but Pepa rejects him and walks away, implying that she has saved his life out of love but that she no longer loves him. The farcical events of the film as a whole, which in part reflect the chaos of Pepa's life, give way finally to a greater sense of stability and order, announced by Pepa's declaration of independence. It is reflected too in her decision to keep the apartment rather than find another one, while the words of the song which accompany the ending of the film point to her recognition of Iván's treachery and thus to her greater prudence in the future:

> It's as if you were on stage . . . faking your pain. . . .
> Don't bother to act . . . I've seen that play before
> . . . I was blinded by your passionate kisses . . .
> You lied coldly . . . but the curtain finally came
> down . . . Play-acting, that's what you do best . . .
> A well executed sham. . . .

Women on the Verge. . ., so utterly different from *Matador*, is in every respect a superb film, revealing to the full Almodóvar's comic talents. In terms of overall structure, it is finely shaped, its individual threads intricately wrought, the seeds of subsequent events sown early and expertly. Within individual sequences, moreover, the variety of comic elements is considerable, ranging from delicate irony, superbly funny dialogue and witty incongruities, to the physical properties of pure farce. In all these respects, *Women on the Verge. . .* is, arguably, the

classic Spanish film comedy, a twentieth-century equivalent of the great comic plays of the seventeenth century.[11] But in the end its comic qualities would count for
little if it had no warmth or heart, a humanity at its centre
with which we can identify. The truth of the matter is
that Pepa in particular, and Candela, Lucía and Marisa
to a lesser extent, emerge as vulnerable, warm, sympathetic human beings whose weaknesses are also ours.
They are not therefore cardboard figures whom we
laugh at, but women of flesh and blood whom we laugh
with precisely because we know them so well. It is the
most healthy kind of laughter.

Notes

1. For a list of awards and prizes, see Nuria Vidal, *El cine
    de Pedro Almodóvar*, Barcelona: Destinolibro, 1990, pp.
    439–441.

2. For Almodóvar's account of the original idea for and
    the subsequent evolution of the plot of *Women on the
    Verge*. . ., see Nuria Vidal, *El cine de Pedro Almodóvar
    . . .*, pp. 257–260.

3. On this point see Nuria Vidal, *El cine de Pedro
    Almodóvar. . .*, pp. 312–315.

4. In Nuria Vidal, *El cine de Pedro Almodóvar. . .*, pp. 266–
    267.

5. Various critics claim that Almodóvar is incapable of
    structuring his films. Antonio Castro, for example, in
    '*Tacones lejanos*, un retorno a *La ley del deseo*', *Dirigido
    por*, October 1991, No. 195, suggests that (the transla-
    tion is my own): '. . . he has shown repeatedly that he
    has some excellent ideas, but he is incapable of sustain-
    ing them for the duration of his films, for they are

distinguished by their complete absence of structure. . . .'
That such a charge could be made against *Women on the
Verge. . .*, given the intricacy of its structure and the
way in which its separate narrative threads are so
cunningly interwoven, is beyond belief.

6. The point has been made in relation to Angel's 'visions'
   in *Matador* that Almodóvar does not distinguish between dream and reality in terms of their presentation
   on the screen. Here he does, precisely in order to
   underscore the artificiality and insincerity of Iván's
   words.

7. Antonio Castro also makes the point that Almodóvar's
   films suffer from the insertion of individual episodes,
   frequent jokes, which 'are badly woven' into the overall structure. As far as *Women on the Verge. . .* is concerned,
   these episodes are clearly in the farcical spirit of the
   film in general.

8. Almodóvar's dialogue is very often beautifully shaped,
   perfectly matched to a given situation, and delightfully
   funny. In *Women on the Verge. . .*, his lines are given
   their full value by some very fine actors.

9. Antonio Castro suggests that Almodóvar's films are
   characterized by an over-reliance on words and that he
   cannot tell a story in visual images alone. This sequence is clearly the answer to that criticism.

10. Misunderstanding of Almodóvar's films seems very
    often to stem from the failure of critics to understand
    that he is juggling often disparate elements in the bold-
    est way. In this respect he is, of course, very much his
    own man and a unique voice in the contemporary
    Spanish film industry.

11. The intricate plots and comic verse of plays like Tirso
    de Molina's *Don Gil en las calzas verdes (Don Gil in the
    Green Breeches)* and Calderón's *La dama duende (The
    Phantom Lady)* immediately come to mind.

High Heels

Almodóvar had originally intended to make *High Heels* after *Law of Desire*, filmed in 1986. A brief consideratin of the plot reveals, however, that it would have been a very different film from that which he eventually made five years later. The story was to take place not in Madrid, the setting of so many of lmodóvar's films, but in the countryside, and would involve two sisters and their mother; a variation, in Almodóvar's words, on Lorca's famous play, *The House of Bernarda Alba*. The two sisters, one a dancer, the other a photographer, had both left home in order to escape their mother's oppressive influence but she refuses to leave them in peace. Thought to have died in a fire — in fact she survives it — the mother continues to pursue one of her daughters for fifteen years and is belieed by her to be a ghost. When the other daughter returns home from a career as a war photographer, the mother's presence in one of her photographs proves that she cannot be a ghost. In the end the photographer daughter shoots the mother, freeing her sister from the belief that she is mad.Almodóvar has observed hat, had he made this film, it would have been 'very surrealist, very Buñuelian, very Lorcan . . . very sureal in an absolutely naturalistic background.' It would also have included songs, notably 'I'm unhappy', with which the film would have commenced, and which would also have been heard subsequently.[1]

In the event, Almodóvar discovered that the conditions for making the projected film were not right and turned instead to a venture which could be filmed without much difficulty in Madrid: *Women on the Verge of a Nervous Breakdown*. When he returned to *High Heels* in 1991, it was to a story which scarcely resembled the one described above. The setting is not the countryside but Madrid itself. The mother-daughter relationship is of a very different kind, the situation reversed in the sense that it is the mother who left home seventeen or so years ago in order to pursue an acting career. In this film, moreover, she haunts her only daughter in a very different sense, the latter clinging desperately to memories and images of her such as that embodied in her songs and the stage performance of a female impersonator. Indeed, it is the daughter-mother relationship in terms of a child's need of, not fear of, the parent which largely dominates the film and places it less in the tradition of Lorca's *La casa de Bernarda Alba* than in that of certain American films such as *Mildred Pierce* and *Stella Dallas*, and Ingmar Bergman's *Autumn Sonata*. It is always possible, of course, that Almodóvar's original story will be made eventually with another title.

Critical reaction to *High Heels* appears to have been less than favourable. Writing in *Sight and Sound*, David Thompson observes that, in trying to make a serious film in which he seeks to engage the audence's emotions more directly, Almodóvar creates 'an absurd plot with its mechanics shamelessly exposed . . . if . . . with this film he is becoming more engaged with dialogue and acting, then his talents are beginning to look sorely stretched. . . .'[2] In an article in the Spanish magazine, *Dirigido por*, Antonio Castro concluded that *High Heels* is a film in which Almodóvar's attempt to create a more orthodox narrative runs parallel with an increasing loss of vigour.[3] In response to such criticism, it can be argued, of course, that Almodóvar himself can always be relied on to undermine and run counter to people's expectations, including those of the reviewers. *High Heels* might well be a much better film than the reactions quoted above suggest.

The title sequence, similar to that of *Women on the Verge. . .* in its overall style, is a minor work of art in itself, pure Almodóvar in that respect. The titles appear over a series of collages composed of shoes, guns, the names of the actors in different colours and portraits in pop-art style of the actors themselves, framed by their names. The effect is that of walking through a picture gallery in which the attention is constantly held by something new, arresting and eye-catching. And the mood of sophisticated elegance is enhanced throughout by Ryuichi Sakamoto's cool, flowing music. Unlike many film directors, Almodóvar frequently uses the title sequence in a quite eye-catching way to arrest the viewer's attention from the very outset.[4]

The film begins with a young woman, Rebecca, played by Victoria Abril, waiting at Madrid airport for the arrival of a plane from Mexico. The first shot of her consists of her reflection in a pane of glass as she looks out through one of the airport windows — a somewhat blurred image which, in effect, announces one of the film's principal themes. In the sense that the image lacks definition, so Rebecca's life lacks definition and true identity. Indeed, she waits at the airport for the return of her mother, Becky, played by Marisa Paredes, who has been away for many years, and on whose account her life has been largely empty. The initial visual image of Rebecca is, in fact, immediately reinforced by another shot in which, behind her, other men and women at the airport are seen reflected in its glass surfaces, all of them shapes and figures lacking identity. In short, Almodóvar uses the physical properties of the airport building in order to project visually, before a word is spoken or a thought revealed, one of his film's major concerns.

The circumstances of Rebecca's childhood are revealed here in two flash-backs. The first concerns a holiday some twenty years ago spent with her mother and one of her mother's lovers, the second an incident two years later, in 1974, the year of her mother's departure to Mexico. Both episodes portray a confused and unhappy child desperate for her mother's love and affection. In the second, indeed, Rebecca is seen switching her stepfather's tranquilizers from one bottle to another, convinced that, if he dies, her mother will be forced to take her with her when she leaves. Despite the success of the plan in one direction — the stepfather drives his car into a tree — it fails in another, for Becky insists that Rebecca stay behind, condemning her to years of unhappiness in which her feelings of betrayal and abandonment are combined with a deep-seated longing for Becky's return. Given this void in Rebecca's life, it is hardly surprising that it should lack definition and identity.

The theme of identity, introduced in relation to Rebecca, is relevant too to Becky herself and, as we shall see, to other characters in the film. Becky is, indeed, a professional actress and singer who has abandoned her role as a mother in order to pursue her career on the stage. As Becky de Páramo she has thus assumed another identity, another life into which all her energies have been directed. Her return to Madrid, moreover, is not undertaken in order to rebuild her relationship with Rebecca but to further her career in a different city, to undertake another challenge. As they leave the airport in the car, Becky informs Rebecca: 'What concerns me is that this city should recognize me.' Noting that her mother seems more interested in the waiting photographers than in her, Rebecca's dis- appointment and bitterness quickly surfaces, in particular in response to Becky's accusation that she did not inform her of her marriage to one of her former lovers, Manuel. It is at this point in the film in which the mother-daughter relationship begins to assume a deeper and more mysterious significance.

Rebecca's feelings for her mother are, to say the least, intense and are revealed in a particular light in relation to two key associations in the film: her marriage to Manuel, mentioned above; and her relationship with the drag artist, Letal. It can be argued that, in marrying Manuel, Becky's one-time lover, Rebecca succeeds in maintaining a kind of contact with her, in preserving something from her mother's past that, like the ear- rings she has kept from almost twenty years ago, helps to fill the void. Her claim that she was unaware of Becky's relationship with Manuel seems dubious to say the least, her later assertion that, in marrying him, she succeeded at least once where her mother failed, is much more likely. But there is more to it than this, for, as Manuel's wife, Rebecca is not only made love to by a man who made love to her mother but, in a sense, becomes her mother by taking her place in his bed. Secondly, her relationship with Letal stems entirely from the fact that, as a drag artist, he specializes in impersonations of Becky. In attending the show over a period of time, Rebecca has witnessed, as it were, her mother's reincarnation, has found a way of replacing her in her absence, of fulfilling a deep-seated need. The song to which Letal mimes as part of his act — 'You will remember our happy days' — is, of course, part of this process, but if we bear in mind that it is essentially a love song containing such lines as, 'You will remember the taste of my kisses', the spectacle of Rebecca serenaded by her 'mother' is certainly ambiguous.[5] But if this is so, what can we make of the dressing room scene which follows?

Rebecca helps Letal undress, removing his tights, unhooking his corset, and remarking in the process: 'I'm delighted you impersonate my mother.' Almost immediately, in one of Almodóvar's most explicit and sensational scenes, Letal begins to make love to her. We are therefore presented with a situation in which Rebecca is being made love to by someone who not merely impersonates her mother but who, over a period of time, she has come to regard as a substitute for her. On one level the sexual encounter is, of course, heterosexual, for Rebecca responds to Letal's considerable muscularity and masculine power. But there is also the strong suggestion that, beneath the surface, there are other, deeper forces and impulses at work. Rebecca, as earlier incidents have confirmed, has a need of and a hunger for her mother which, Almodóvar suggests, goes into territory she would not admit to, but which, in the relationship with Letal, including the sexual side of things, finds an outlet. This is one of Almodóvar's most provocative and fascinating scenes, rich in ambiguity, and if it is explicit in its sexuality it is less to do with his desire to be outrageous, as many critics would imply, than with his concern to reveal the deep, even incestuous nature of the daughter-mother bond.[6] It is surely no accident that, in response to Manuel's sarcastic question as to the gender of the name Letal, Letal should reply that one can take it as one wants, it is both masculine and feminine. In the sense that the reply is deliberately ambiguous, it serves

also to underline the ambiguity of Rebecca's relationship with Letal and thus with her mother.

The first third of *High Heels*, dominated by the mother-
daughter relationship, is almost entirely serious and
has few of the comic touches so often associated with
Almodóvar. A month later, moreover, Manuel is found
murdered, and a film so far concerned with questions
of relationship and identity moves into the equally
serious territory of the murder mystery, introducing
Judge Domínguez as the police investigator.[7] In a pre-
liminary interview with Rebecca, Becky, and Isabel, a
television interpreter for the deaf and hard-of-hearing,
it is revealed that all three women visited Manuel on
the night of the murder and that both Becky and Isabel
have recently been his lovers — Isabel, indeed, on the
night of his death. To this extent the sequence is one
which is highly fraught, revealing, for example, Becky's
sense of guilt and Rebecca's strained relationship with
Manuel, as well as her fluctuating emotions on returning to the house on the night in question. On the other
hand, there are comic hints and undertones in the fact
that all three women are the dead man's lovers and
that, sitting side by side, they are obliged to listen to
their rivals' confessions. In many ways it is a situation
Buñuel himself might well have engineered.

The serious, even melodramatic surface and the comic
possibilities of the sequence just described characterize
to a large extent the rest of the film, revealing very
clearly Almodóvar's love of juxtaposing, often at great
risk, contrasting elements and styles. It is a process
which is illustrated particularly well by Rebecca's reading
of the television news. The sequence begins on a serious note with Rebecca driving to the television studio
immediately after Manuel's funeral. She is in a state of
considerable anguish, tears rolling down her cheeks,

her grief accompanied on the sound-track by slow, heavy and lugubrious music. It is the style we might associate with Hollywood melodramas of the 1940s and 50s. The newsreading proper also begins seriously with an item about farmers protesting, Isabel seated alongside Rebecca and interpreting her words in appropriate sign language for the benefit of the deaf. Initially, then, the situation is one of pure formality and cool objectivity, everything under control. When, however, Rebecca begins to report Manuel's funeral, she also begins to abandon the script and inject personal comments. Informing the public that the autopsy reveals Manuel to have made love just before his death, Rebecca interjects: 'I can only say that it wasn't with me.' The traditional formality of the tele-cast is thus undermined by the revelation of personal and intimate details.[8] Secondly, the technical staff are thrown into increasing disarray and Isabel's efforts to communicate to the deaf made even more uncertain. And when, finally, Rebecca confesses on-screen to the murder of Manuel, Isabel, at a total loss but not completely forgetting her sign-language, can only point at Rebecca, stabbing her finger in her direction. Throughout the sequence Rebecca herself behaves in a completely serious way. The comic element is therefore created by the surrounding circumstances — by the way in which the communication of objective fact dissolves step by step into personal confession and by the reaction of others to it. For the first time in the film, then, the serious and often melodramatic tone dissolves into farce, as if Almodóvar, having assumed a serious expression, cannot hold it for very long. If for some the process is disconcerting, it should be borne in mind that Spanish writers and creative artists in general have, over the centuries, always been aware of the close juxtaposition in life of the comic and the serious, of laughter and tears, and have sought to express it in their work. In this respect Almodóvar is one in a long tradition which includes Cervantes, Lope de Vega, Calderón, Francisco de Quevedo, Goya, Valle-Inclán, Lorca and Buñuel.[9]

The validity of this point is underlined by the fact that the farcical telecast is followed by two highly emotional and dramatic sequences which are themselves separated by a light-hearted dance routine. In the first of the two dramatic sequences Becky gives her first concert in Madrid since her return, while Rebecca languishes in prison, listening to her mother on the radio. The tone of the episode is set at the very outset when Becky kisses the stage, leaving upon it the imprint of her lips. There is in this effusive and very 'show-biz' gesture a sentimentality which is compounded a little later when a single tear shed by Becky falls to the stage beside the imprint of her lips. The two images, lips and tears, encapsulate the essence of the sequence in a style which is again that of pop-art and which is, to that extent, stylized and somewhat facile. The song sung by Becky and dedicated to Rebecca — 'Think of me' — is in itself markedly romantic and sentimental, and is given a performance by Becky which is strongly emotional. Indeed, as she listens to the song in prison, Rebecca becomes more and more distraught, and the sequence as a whole both sentimental and melodramatic. But if there is a strong element of self-indulgence on Almodóvar's part, it is also clear that not only does he cultivate it deliberately, controlling it from beginning to end, but that at any moment he is likely to undermine it.

The second sequence concerns a meeting between Rebecca and Becky which focuses crucially on their relationship and brings to the fore once more the central theme of identity. The meeting begins badly with Becky revealing that she has come not of her own free will but only at the insistence of Judge Domínguez, and becomes a sustained accusation by Rebecca of her mother's indifference towards her over the years. She compares her position to that of the daughter in Ingmar Bergman's *Autumn Sonata* in which the girl feels, and is often made to feel, inferior to her mother, an accomplished pianist. Insisting that their own relationship is essentially similar, Rebecca informs Becky that she has spent her life trying to live up to her. Only in marrying Manuel has she ever bettered her, and even then, on her return, Becky has humiliated her by sleeping with him. The sequence ends with Rebecca walking out, vowing never to forgive her mother, and is distinguished throughout by its powerful emotional charge. Some critics have seen the deliberate allusion to Bergman's film as evidence of Almodóvar shooting himself in the foot and suggested that a comparison merely draws attention to the inferior quality of his own work.[10] The truth of the matter is, firstly, that, considered in its own right, the sequence is extremely powerful, its emotions strong and immediate in a typically Spanish way, and, secondly, that Almodóvar's approach, whatever the influences, is unmistakably his own. The problem appears to lie in the fact that many critics cannot understand his methods, find them disconcerting and are consequently scathing in their comments. But for Almodóvar himself surprise is all.

The dance routine, placed between the sequences described above, makes the point. In the exercise yard of the prison, the women prisoners break suddenly into a choreographed dance with musical accompaniment, as if *High Heels* were a Hollywood musical. The episode has, of course, been seized upon by critics for its irrelevance to the rest of the film, as well as for its disruption of the narrative. In fact, it is an incongruous and essentially comic scene and in that sense perfectly in accord with other moments in the film. We do not expect prisoners to perform a stylized dance in an exercise yard any more than we expect a television newsreader to admit to murder in the course of reading the news. Almodóvar subverts our expectations in both cases, revealing again his predilection for surprise and ambush. In order to respond in any constructive sense to his style, the critic must at least have an open mind.

The last third or so of the film highlights the theme of identity in a number of ways. Released from prison because there is not enough evidence to keep her there, Rebecca, now pregnant, is informed by Judge Domínguez that Letal wishes to speak to her and is urged by him to visit the club. The beginning of Letal's act is used, significantly, to juxtapose three images in a way which places the emphasis very firmly on the question of identity in relation to the Rebecca-Becky-Letal triangle. The first image is that of Becky in her dressing room, which becomes a close-up of a poster of her in performance, which is set side by side, in the very same shot, with a close-up of Letal as he begins his impersonation of Becky. What is more, Rebecca is now listening to Letal singing precisely the same song — 'Think of me' — that Becky previously sang when Rebecca was in prison. The overlapping of the identities of Becky and Letal is thus made even more specific. The line in the song — 'I worship your divine image' — also seems significant, for it echoes Rebecca's earlier assertion that, as a child, she adored her mother. In a variety of ways, then, the deeper implications of the mother-daughter relationship become even more intriguing, and all the more so in the light of the fact that Becky's 'image', Letal, is in all probability the father of Rebecca's child. But there is more to it than this, for in the dressing room after his performance and when, unknown to him, Rebecca has entered, Letal is suddenly revealed to be none other than Judge Domínguez. In other words, Judge Domínguez is Letal who is, in turn, Becky. It is an astonishing moment, and when the Judge asks Rebecca to marry him, her reply — 'Marry who? You, Letal? Who?' — not only exposes her confusion but points to the issues of identity and gender which lie at the heart of the film. As far as Judge Domínguez is concerned, he claims the drag act to be a disguise which he has assumed in order to investigate the murder of a transvestite at the club some months previously, but can we really believe him? On the one hand, he evidently enjoys the performance. On the other, much of his private life appears to be spent at home with a mad mother whom he waits on hand and foot and who loses herself in the fantasy world of celebrities' lives contained in her photograph albums. Who knows, then, to what extent the Judge, suffocated by his home life, himself seeks escape in a world of make-believe and sexual fantasy?[11] The degree to which the notion of assuming other roles and identities pervades *High Heels* is, on consideration, very extensive. Rebecca, as a television newsreader, performs an act, submerging her real identity in that of a public figure. Becky has performed for years, to the point where her stage act has taken over her life, obliterating her role as mother. And Letal, as we have seen, performs an act in which he conceals not merely his identity but, in a sense, his sex. In the context of all this, the significance of make-up and costume in the film is all important. At different times Rebecca, Becky and Letal are all seen in front of mirrors transforming themselves or being transformed into someone else. Who, then, is the real person beneath the mask? The question reverberates throughout the film.

If the Judge's exposure poses that question, it also plunges the film into farce. Consider the state of affairs consequent upon the Judge's revelation of his identity: the murder of Manuel is being investigated by Judge Domínguez who imprisons Rebecca on suspicion of that murder. Just prior to this, Rebecca has been made pregnant by Letal, who impersonates her mother, and who, it is subsequently revealed, is in reality the Judge himself. The Judge who is investigating the murder of Rebecca's husband is thus responsible for the pregnancy of his widow, who is also the suspected murderess. And finally, this prominent upholder of law and order, unaware that Rebecca is truly guilty, ends up marrying the perpetrator of the crime, the mother of his child. It is a story whose ingenious twists and turns rivals, as does *Women on the Verge. . .* many a Spanish seventeenth-century comedy, not to mention many a twentieth-century English farce. Once more, then, the serious aspects of the film, involving those questions of role and identity mentioned above, are accompanied by comic and subversive undercurrents, two opposites juxtaposed, played and juggled with in the most unexpected way.

The mixture is sustained in the film's concluding scenes. Rebecca, already astounded by her discovery of Letal's real identity, is further shocked when she hears on television the report of Becky's heart attack. The announcement introduces a highly dramatic sequence in which Rebecca and the Judge rush to the hospital and which, in characteristic Hollywood fashion, is structured thereafter around a tearful reunion and bedside confession. Asked by Becky to tell her the truth — the Judge is outside the room — Rebecca confesses to Manuel's murder. When the Judge appears, Becky informs him that she committed the crime, thereby removing suspicion from her daughter. Almodóvar, of course, milks the scene for its stagey, melodramatic qualities, but, since we know what the Judge does not — that Rebecca is the murderess, whom he is soon to marry — leaves us to savour its comic implications. The sequence ends, moreover, with a truly Buñuelian touch. When a priest enters solemnly to take Becky's confession, she informs him that, although she did not do it, she has just confessed to the Judge to Manuel's murder. The priest then engages her in a portentous conversation about lying and confessing which is not only incongruous in the context of Becky's tenuous hold on life itself, but which becomes in its pomposity a genuine self-parody.[12]

Becky is subsequently taken home to die. The journey in the ambulance, in which she requests from Rebecca the precise details of the murder, is in one sense full of pathos but is full of comic touches. Indeed, the spectacle of Rebecca recounting the murder in an ambulance to her mother who is wearing an oxygen-mask is not without a degree of black humour. There are also some delightfully comic lines. Demanding to know precisely how Manuel died, Becky earnestly enquires: 'did he fall backwards or did he fall forwards?' At the end of Rebecca's account, moreover, she gives her daughter advice which, in the circumstances, is quite hilarious: 'Rebecca, you'll have to learn to solve your problems with men in some other way!' Again, at home in the final sequences there is a comic edge to the two women muttering prayers outside Becky's bedroom, as well as in her insistence on putting her fingerprints on the murder weapon before she dies. If there is a final Hollywood-style reconciliation between mother and daughter and an emotional ending capped by heavy music, this does not preclude Almodóvar's underlying sense of irony, so typically Spanish, which allows him to distance himself from his material sufficiently in order to be able to smile at it.

In relation to *Matador* and *Women on the Verge. . .*, *High Heels* contains both the seriousness of the former and the comedy of the latter. Indeed, in *Matador* there are, despite its predominantly serious character, richly comic moments — consider Eva's worldly mother, Pilar — and in *Women on the Verge. . .* serious comments within its overall comic manner. From that point of view, *High Heels*, not unexpectedly, reveals all the Almodóvar hallmarks. Much has been made of his efforts to make a 'serious' film, and to some extent this is true. But in the end, as in earlier films, *High Heels* is a work in which different stylistic elements are cleverly and deliberately mixed and which should be seen as a heady and stimulating cocktail.[13]

Notes

1. See Nuria Vidal, *El cine de Pedro Almodóvar*, Barcelona: Destinolibro, 1990, pp. 249–256. Almodóvar describes in great detail the plot of his proposed film. What is quite striking here is his indebtedness to Spanish tradition, in particular Lorca and Buñuel.

2. *Sight and Sound*, Winter 1992, p. 61.

3. 'Tacones lejanos, un retorno a La ley del deseo', *Dirigido por*, October 1991, p. 25.

4. The statement of one of the film's principal themes at the very outset suggests a concern with ideas and structure for which Almodóvar is not always given credit. The same concern is also evident in the other films studied here.

5. The songs in the film seem to stem from Almodóvar's original project which would have opened with 'I'm unhappy.' See the opening paragraph of this chapter.

6. David Thompson, *Sight and Sound*. . ., p. 62, describes it, condescendingly, as a 'token awkward grapple.'

7. David Thompson, *Sight and Sound*. . ., p. 62, refers to Almodóvar's own description of *High Heels* as 'a touch melodramatic, at times close to terror or *film noir*.'

8. Almodóvar evidently regards television advertisement as a rich source of comedy. Consider the hilarious television advertisement for 'Omo' in *Women on the Verge*. . ., as well as his use of his mother as a television newsreader in the same film.

9. The incongruities of *High Heels* can be compared, for example, with those of Buñuel's *The Discreet Charm of the Bourgeoisie* in which the attempts of the bourgeois group to eat their meal are interrupted by such bizarre events as the death of the restaurant owner and military manoeuvres.

10. See David Thomson, *Sight and Sound*. . ., p. 62: 'Here it has the doubly distancing effect of not only making one think of the superiority of Bergman's treatment of the same theme, but also of Almodóvar's characters' inability to achieve their own sense of identity outside a world of devoted reference. . . .' For any critic to consider a comparison between Almodóvar and Bergman, given their differences of nationality and culture, is quite absurd. It almost seems a case of critics making fools of themselves by rising to Almodóvar's bait.

11. The son condemned to a life at home with an oppressive mother is also, of course, a central theme of *Matador*, while in *Women on the Verge. . .* Carlos's mother, Lucía, is quite mad.

12. Consider the sanctimonious and self-satisfied priests of such films as Buñuel's *Nazarín* and *Tristana*.

13. The title *High Heels* is not an accurate translation of the Spanish original, *Tacones lejanos*, which means 'distant heels'. At the end of the film Rebecca describes how, as a child, she always felt comforted when she heard the sound of her mother's distant heels approaching. The Spanish title therefore expresses very clearly the importance of the mother-daughter relationship to the film, which the English title does not.

Conclusion

No study of Spain in the twentieth century, be it of politics, society or any of the art forms, can escape the conclusion that the Civil War has been the one single event that has had the most profound effect on the thinking and the attitudes of Spaniards in general. In that respect the twelve films studied here possess, for all their differences, the kind of inter-dependence and inter-relationship which is to be found elsewhere, say, in that body of American work at whose centre lies the exploration of the American Dream. Between the four Spanish film directors in question there is thus both a clear link and a marked sense of continuity. Moving from one film to another, the critic forms an impression of a body of work behind which lies the painful history of a nation and which only now, in the films of Almodóvar, is beginning to throw off that legacy.

The films are linked, first of all, by their themes. Buñuel had left Spain before the beginning of the War but understood much better than most the character of his native country: its clinging to tradition, the influence of the Catholic church, the significance of social status, name and honour, the repression of sexual freedom, the importance of machismo and the subservient role of women. In both his Mexican and Spanish films, and his later French films, he would produce brilliant and arresting variations on one or more of those themes whose roots lay in his understanding of Spain itself. Saura and Erice, the former thirty-two, the latter forty years younger than Buñuel, would develop precisely the same themes in the markedly different circumstances of the aftermath of the War, which had merely served to strengthen the hold of all those things attacked by the older man. Between Buñuel's *Tristana*, set before the War, Erice's *The Spirit of the Beehive*, during it, and Saura's *Raise Ravens*, after it, there is thus a striking similarity in the fact that in each of them the child or young woman is seen to be shaped, even crippled, by the world in which she lives. Similarly, the stripping away of the masks of formal elegance and social etiquette in Buñuel's *The Exterminating Angel* is at bottom no different from the exposure of hypocrisy and infidelity behind the façade of middle-class morality in Saura's *Raise Ravens*. And if Tristana achieves her freedom from male oppression at the terrible cost of a growing bitterness, she is very much a soul-mate of Carmen who pays for it with her life. Of the four film directors, only Almodóvar deals with themes which, in the sense that they are often the opposite of those mentioned above (sexual freedom, gay relationships and the like) reflect the fact that the transition from dictatorship to democracy has indeed put paid to the aftermath of the War.

If the themes of the films are often similar, their variety is very striking. This is sometimes, of course, in the nature of the films themselves. What could be more different than the harsh realism of Saura's *The Hunt* and the stylized beauty of the choreographed sequences in the same director's *Carmen*, or the rural backwardness of Buñuel's *Viridiana* and the city elegance of Almodóvar's *Women on the Verge of a Nervous Breakdown*? On the other hand, each of the four film-makers has a very distinctive, personal style. To study the films of Buñuel is to become aware of a master of narrative and of someone for whom the surface of the film is often a pointer to the inner lives of its characters. His films have, in terms of their movement, a sense of logic and progression, of being almost organic, which are the hallmarks of a film-maker whose instinct and touch are absolutely sure. In certain respects Saura's style is not unlike that of his acknowledged master: an apparent realism which, on examination, is seen to be both selective and symbolic, the surface of the film a mirror of greater, more universal issues. On the other hand, the trajectory of Saura's cinema is one in which a greater complexity is very evident, not least in the search for new forms — dance and opera — to express old themes, although, like Buñuel, he eschews all tricks and gimmickry. This sobriety, a characteristic of Spanish culture throughout the ages, is typical too of the films of Erice, although the unfussy narrative style is accompanied here by a highly distinctive 'poetic' quality: the presentation of objective reality accompanied by music, the sounds of nature, even silence, all of which says more about the characters in a particular setting than about the setting itself. As for Almodóvar, nothing would appear at first sight to be more removed from the often eccentric, off-beat, gaudy world of his films than the simple sobriety of Buñuel, Saura and Erice. Yet in terms of style and technique, of shooting and putting the film together, he has much in common with them. If the surface of the films is that of the modern commercial world with its fashions, furnishings and colour, the manner is often that of Buñuel, the rhythm of the films fast, simple, direct, the technique straightforward. Almodóvar has, indeed, resisted the lure of Hollywood, revealing that his roots are essentially Spanish. It is this quality, this Spanishness which gives the films studied here, as well as their makers, the feeling of belonging to a family.

Bibliography

GENERAL

Besas, Peter *Behind the Spanish Lens*, Denver: Arden Press, 1985.

Castro, Antonio *El cine español en el banquillo*, Valencia: Fernando Torres Ed., 1974.

Evans, Peter and Fiddian, Robin *Challenges to Authority: Fiction and Film in Contemporary Spain*, London: Tamesis, 1988.

García Fernández, Emilio C.*Historia ilustrada del cine español*, Madrid: Planeta, 1985.

Hernández Les, Juan & Gato, Miguel *El cine de autor en España*, Madrid: Miguel Castellote, 1978.

Hernández, Marta*El aparato cinematográfico español*, Barcelona: Akal, 1976.

Higginbotham, Virginia *Spanish Film Under Franco*, Austin: University of Texas Press, 1988.

Hopewell, John *Out of the Past, Spanish Cinema After Franco*, London: British Film Institute, 1986.

Larraz, Emmanuel *El cine español*, Paris: Mason et Cie Ed., 1973.

Maqua, Javier & Pérez Merinero, Carlos *Cine español, ida y vuelta*, Valencia: Fernando Torres Ed., 1976.

Molina Foix, Vicente *New Cinema in Spain*, London: British Film Institute, 1977.

Torres, Augusto M. (ed.) *Spanish Cinema 1896–1983*, Madrid: Ministerio de Cultura, Instituto de Cine, 1986.

Vizcaíno Casas, F. *Historia y anécdota del cine español*, Madrid: Ediciones Adra, 1976.

LUIS BUÑUEL

Aranda, J. Francisco *Luis Buñuel, biografía crítica*, Barcelona: Editorial Lumen, 1969; *Luis Buñuel: a Critical Biography*, trans. David Robinson, London: Secker & Warburg, 1975.

Aub, Max *Conversaciones con Buñuel*, Madrid: Aguilar, 1985.

Buache, Freddy *Luis Buñuel*, Lausanne: La Cité, 1970. *The Cinema of Luis Buñuel*, trans. Peter Graham, London & New York: Tantivy-Barnes, 1973.

Buñuel, Luis *My Last Breath*, London: Fontana, 1985.

Durgnat, Raymond *Luis Buñuel*, London: Studio Vista, 1964.

Edwards, Gwynne *The Discreet Art of Luis Buñuel*, London and Boston: Marion Boyars, 1982.

Grange, Frèdèric (with Rebolledo, Carlos) *Luis Buñuel*, Paris: Editions Universitaires, 1964.

Higginbotham, Virginia*Luis Buñuel*, Boston: Twayne, 1979.

Kyrou, Ado*Luis Buñuel*, Paris: Editions Seghers, 1962.

Mellen, Joan (ed) *The World of Luis Buñuel: Essays in Criticism*, New York: Oxford University Press, 1978.

Sánchez Vidal, Agustín *Luis Buñuel*, Madrid: Ediciones JC, 1984.

CARLOS SAURA

Brasó, Enrique *Carlos Saura*, Madrid: Taller Ediciones JB, 1974.

Hidalgo, Manuel *Carlos Saura*, Madrid: Ediciones JC, 1981.

Oms, Marcel *Carlos Saura*, Paris: Edilig, 1981.

Sánchez Vidal, Agustínn *El cine de Carlos Saura*, Zaragoza: Caja de Ahorros de la Inmaculada, 1988.

VICTOR ERICE

Evans, Peter'*El espíritu de la colmena*: the Monster, the Place of the Father and Growing up in the Dictatorship', *Vida Hispánica*, Autumn 1982, XXXI, no. 3.

Fernández Santos, Angel '33 preguntas eruditas sobre *El Sur*', *Casablanca*, nos 31–32, July–August 1983, pp. 55–58.

Molina Foix, Vicente'*La guerra detrás de la ventana*', *Revista de Occidente*, no. 53, October 1985; 'Victor Erice: El cine de los supervivientes' *Mayo*, no. 12, September 1983.

Riley, E.C.'The Story of Ana in *El espíritu de la colmena*', *Bulletin of Hispanic Studies*, LXI, 1984.

Smith, Paul Julian'Whispers and Rapture', *Sight and Sound*, No. 4, 1993, pp. 28–29.

PEDRO ALMODÓVAR

Blanco, Francisco ('Boquerini') *Pedro Almodóvar*, Madrid: Ediciones JC, 1989.

García de León, María Antonia and Maldonado, Teresa *Pedro Almodóvar, la otra España cañi*, Ciudad Real: Biblioteca de Autores y Temas Manchegos, 1989.

Smith, Paul Julian *Laws of Desire*, Cambridge: Cambridge University Press, 1992.

Vidal, Nuria *El cine de Pedro Almodóvar*, Barcelona: Ediciones Destinolibro, 1988.

Index

Abril, Victoria 200

Almodóvar, Pedro 10, 20–23, 215, 216, 217
 High Heels 198–214
 Labyrinth of Passion 182
 Law of Desire 179, 182, 198
 Matador 164–180, 182, 183, 186, 195, 197, 212, 214
 Pepi, Luci, Bom and All the Other Girls on the Heap 22, 23, 182
 Sex, Easy Come Easy Go 21
 The Dream or the Star 21
 The Fall of Sodom 21
 Two Whores, or a Love Story which Ends in Marriage 21
 Women on the Verge of a Nervous Breakdown 181–197, 199, 200, 210, 212, 216

The Apartment (Wilder) 182

Aranda, Francisco 24, 38, *54*

Autumn Sonata (Bergman) 199, 207

Ay, Carmela! (Sinisterra) 116

Azcona, Rafael 86

Banderas, Antonio 181

Bergamín, José 43

Bergman, Ingmar 102, 199, 207

Bernarda Alba 65, 169

Bizet, George 101, 102, 104, 105, 106–107, 109, 110, 111, 112, 113, 114, 115

Blood Wedding (García Lorca) 17, 158, 176

'Blue Moon' 156

Bosch, Hieronymus 33

Breughel 33

Buñuel, Luis 9, 10, 11–14, 16, 17, 19, 20, 23, 71, 72, 73, *84*, 110, *131*, 144, 165, 169, 171, 198, 206, 211, 215, 216, 217
 Belle de Jour 39, 42, 44, 55
 Diary of a Chambermaid 13, *54*, 55, 68
 L'Age d'or 12, 13, 26, 38, 41, 42, 44, 45, 46, 48, *54*, 73
 Nazarín 13, 27, 33, 34, *69*, 144, 214
 Simon of the Desert 13, 27
 That Obscure Object of Desire 53
 The Castaways of Providence Street 43
 The Discreet Charm of the Bourgeoisie 13, 42, 43, 44, 45, 48, 53
 The Exterminating Angel 14, 41–54 55, 56, 58, 216
 The Young and the Damned (Los olvidados) 50
 Tristana 14, 55–71, 110, *214*, 216
 Un Chien andalou 12, 13, *54*, 133–134, 166
 Viridiana 10, 13, 24, 26–40, 44, 51, 55, 56, 58, 59, 61, 67, 68, *179*, 216

Calderón de la Barca, Pedro 42, *69*, 158, *197*, 206

Carmen (Bizet) 102

Castro, Antonio *196*, *197*, 199,

Cat People (Tourneur) 165

Cervantes 34, 42, 60, *146*, 206

Chaplin, Geraldine 92

Christ 36, *40*, *121*, 169

Cocteau, Jean 182

Communist Party 11
Crawford, Joan 184
Cuadra, Pilar de 55, 162

Dalí, Salvador 177
Da Vinci, Leonardo 36, 40
Diario de Barcelona 55
Díaz de Mendívil, Santiago 87
Dirigido por 196, 199
'The Disasters of War' (Goya) 79
Don Quixote 34, 69, 131, *146*
Duel in the Sun (Vidor) 165, 172
Durgnat, Raymond 24, *39, 40*, 41

Engels, Friedrich 42
Erice, Victor 7, 10, 18– 20, 87, 165,
  215, 216, 217
  Los desafíos (The Challenges) 132
  The South 19, 148–163, 172
  The Spirit of the Beehive 19, 20, 87,
  132–147, 148, 154, 160, 161, *162*,
  216, 217
Evans, Peter *100*, *114*, *147*, 149,
  154, *162*, *163*

Fanny and Alexander (Bergman) 102
Fernández Santos, Angel 148
Ferrero, Jesús 164, 165
Fiddian, Robin *114*, 149, 154, *162*,
  163
Frankenstein (Whale) 132–133, 148
Frankenstein, Dr 132, 135, 136,
  137, 141, 142, 143
Frankenstein's monster 19, 20, 132,
  133, 136, 139, 140, 142, 144, 145
Freud, Sigmund 17, *69*, *163*

The Garden of Earthly Delights
  (Bosch) 33
García Lorca, Federico 17, 61, 65,
  94, 101, 158, 176, *180*, 198, 199,
  206
Glaessner, Verina 165

God, the Only Good Fortune
  (Caldéron) 42
Golding, William 43
Goya, Francisco 33, 42, 79, 111, 206
Gutiérrez Aragón, Manuel 72

Hallelujah Chorus (Handel) 37
Hayden, Sterling 184
Helévy 102
Hinojosa, José María 71
Hitchcock, Alfred 148, 149
The House of Bernarda Alba (García
  Lorca) 61, 94, 198, 199
Hoyos, Cristina 105

'The Jealous Extremaduran'
  (Cervantes) 60
Johnny Guitar (Ray) 184
Jones, Jennifer 172

Karloff, Boris 132

Lampreave, Chus 181, 191
The Last Supper (Da Vinci) 36, 40
Laura (Preminger) 149
Lazarillo de Tormes 59
Le Monde 55
Life is a Dream (Calderón) 158
Lope de Vega 206
Lord of the Flies (Golding) 43
Lucía, Paco de 104

Machado, Antonio 74, 119
MacLaine, Shirley 182
Marcorelles, Louis 55
Maura, Carmen 120, 181, 182
Mayo, Alfredo 76
Meihac 102
Mérimée, Prosper 101, 102, 104,
  105, 106, 107, 108, 111, 112, *115*
Mildred Pierce (Curtiz) 199

Nuestro Cine 55, *84*, 132

Opus Dei 169
O'Toole, Lawrence 166, *179*

Pajares, Andrés 120
Peck, Gregory 172
Pérez Galdós, Benito 42, 56, 60
Piedra, Emiliano 101

Querejeta, Elías 71, 132, *146*, 148
Quevedo, Francisco de 206

Ray, Nicholas 149
Rebel Without a Cause (Ray) 149
Rebecca (Hitchock) 149
Robinson Crusoe 43, 52
Romeo and Juliet (Shakespeare) 149
Rosi, Francesco 101

Sakamoto, Ryuichi 200
Sanchís Sinisterra, José 116, 117
Sancho Panza 34, 125
Santos Fontenla, César 55, 72
Saura, Carlos 10, 14–18, 132, 134, 145, 215, 216, 217
  Ana and the Wolves 16
  Ay, Carmela! 15, 116–131
  Blood Wedding 17, 101, 113, *115*
  Carmen 17, 18, 101–115, 216
  Cousin Angélica 15, 86
  El Dorado 16, 19
  Lament for a Bandit (Llanto por un bandido) 71

Love the Magician (El amor brujo) 101
Raise Ravens 16, 18, 19, 86–100, 110, *130*, 140, *147*, 149, 216
The Drifters (Los golfos) 71
The Hunt 16, 18, 19, 71–85, 98, 110, *130*, 134, 145, *147*, 216
Serrano, Julieta 181
Shadow of a Doubt (Hitchcock) 148, 149
Sight and Sound 25, 165, *178*, *179*, 199, *212*, *213*
St John of the Cross 27
Stella Dallas (Vidor) 149, 199
Suárez, Adolfo 87

Tess of the D'Urbervilles (Hardy) 149
Thompson, David 199, *213*
Torrent, Ana 87, 140

Unamuno, Miguel de 137
An Unmarried Woman (Mazursky) 149

Valle-Inclán, Ramón del 206
Vermeer 151
La Voix humaine (Cocteau) 182

Whale, James 132, 148
Wilder, Billy 182
The Woman in the Window (Lang) 149
Wuthering Heights (Brontë) 149